A Gift for:

From:

Everyday Blessings

Inspirational Thoughts from the Published Works of

MAX LUCADO

J. COUNTRYMAN

Nashville, Tennessee
www.jcountryman.com
A division of Thomas Nelson, Inc.
www.thomasnelson.com

Published by J. Countryman, a division of Thomas Nelson, Inc, Nashville, Tennessee 37214.

Compiled and edited by Terri Gibbs

Editorial Supervision: Karen Hill, Administrative Editor for Max Lucado

Designed by UDG|DesignWorks, Sisters, Oregon.

ISBN: 14041-0042-3

Printed and bound in Belgium

*God always
applauds what
is right.*

God is our protection and our strength.
He always helps in times of trouble.

PSALM 46:12

Ever feel as if you need to get away?
So did Jesus. (Mark 1:35).

Ever have so many demands that you can't
stop for lunch? He can relate. (Mark 6:31). . . .

Do your friends ever let you down? When
Christ needed help, his friends dozed off.
(Matt. 26:40). . . .

When you turn to him for help, he runs
to you to help. Why? He knows how you feel.
He's been there. . . .

So go to him.

MAX LUCADO

The heavens tell the glory of God.

PSALM 19:1

*I*f you were the only person on earth,
the earth would look exactly the same.
The Himalayas would still have their drama
and the Caribbean would still have its charm.
The sun would still nestle behind the Rockies
in the evenings and spray light on the desert
in the mornings. If you were the sole pilgrim
on this globe, God would not diminish its
beauty one degree.

Because he did it all for you.

I call to you in times of trouble, because you will answer me.

PSALM 86:7

You can talk to God because God listens. Your voice matters in heaven. He takes you very seriously. When you enter His presence, the attendants turn to you to hear your voice. No need to fear that you will be ignored. Even if you stammer or stumble, even if what you have to say impresses no one, it impresses God, and He listens.

MAX LUCADO

Thank GOD! He deserves your thanks. His love never quits.

PSALM 136:1, THE MESSAGE

*I*f I know that one of the privileges of fatherhood is to comfort a child, then why am I so reluctant to let my heavenly Father comfort me?

Why do I think he wouldn't want to hear about my problems? ("They are puny compared to people starving in India.") Why do I think he is too busy for me?

If we love one another, God lives
in us and his love is made complete in us.
1 JOHN 4:12, NIV

God loves you. Personally. Powerfully. Passionately. Others have promised and failed. But God has promised and succeeded. He loves you with an unfailing love. And His love—if you will let it—can fill you and leave you with a love worth giving.

MAX LUCADO

I know those I have chosen.

JOHN 13:18

Would you choose a wanted murderer to lead a nation out of bondage? Would you call upon a fugitive to carry the Ten Commandments? God did. . . . Called his name through a burning bush. Scared old Moses right out of his shoes! . . .

The reassuring lesson is clear. God . . . uses people to change the world. *People!* Not saints or superhumans or geniuses, but people.

Though he was God, he did not
demand and cling to his rights as God.
PHILIPPIANS 2:6, NLT

Need more patience? Drink from the patience of God (2 Pet. 3:9). Is generosity an elusive virtue? Then consider how generous God has been with you (Rom. 5:8). Having trouble putting up with ungrateful relatives or cranky neighbors? God puts up with you when you act the same. "He is kind to the ungrateful and wicked" (Luke 6:35, NIV).

Can't we love like this?

In Christ there is all of God in a human body.

COLOSSIANS 2:9, TLB

Jesus was not a godlike man, nor a manlike God. He was God-man. . . . The maker of the world with a bellybutton. . . .

What do we do with such a person? We applaud men for doing good things. We enshrine God for doing great things. But when a man does God things?

One thing is certain, we can't ignore him. Why would we want to?

Ask, and God will give to you.
Search, and you will find.
MATTHEW 7:7

Countless copies of Scripture sit unread on bookshelves and nightstands simply because people don't know how to read it. What can we do to make the Bible real in our lives?

The clearest answer is found in the words of Jesus. "Ask and God will give it to you." The first step in understanding the Bible is asking God to help us.

Christ died for sins once for all,
the righteous for the unrighteous, to bring you to God.

1 PETER 3:18, NIV

The path of righteousness is a narrow, winding trail up a steep hill. At the top of the hill is a cross. At the base of the cross are bags. Countless bags full of innumerable sins. Calvary is the compost pile of guilt. Would you like to leave yours there as well?

The Son of Man came to find lost people and save them.

LUKE 19:10, NCV

God will do what it takes—whatever it takes—to bring his children home.

He is the shepherd in search of His lamb. His legs are scratched, His feet are sore, and His eyes are burning. He scales the cliffs and traverses the fields. He explores the caves. He cups His hands to His mouth and calls into the canyon.

And the name He calls is yours.

MAX LUCADO

Accept one another, then, just as Christ accepted you.

ROMANS 15:7, NIV

Grace makes three proclamations.

Dealing with my sins is God's responsibility. I repent, I confess, but only God can forgive. (And he does.) . . .

Dealing with my neighbor is God's responsibility. I must speak; I must pray. But only God can convince. (And he does.) . . .

God loves me and makes me his child. God loves my neighbor and makes him my brother.

I will come back and take you to be with me.

JOHN 14:3

We don't know when Christ will come for us. We don't know how he will come for us. And, we really don't even know why he would come for us. . . . Most of what we have is faith. Faith that he has ample space and a prepared place and, at the right time, he will come so that we can be where he is.

He will do the taking. It's up to us to do the trusting.

MAX LUCADO

*Go after a life of love as if
your life depended on it—because it does.*

1 CORINTHIANS 14:1, THE MESSAGE

*L*oosen up. Don't you have some people to hug, rocks to skip, or lips to kiss? . . . Someday you are going to retire; why not today?

Not retire from your job, just retire from your attitude. Honestly, has complaining ever made the day better? Has grumbling ever paid the bills? Has worrying about tomorrow ever changed it?

Let someone else run the world for a while.

What is impossible with men is possible with God.

LUKE 18:27, NIV

The rich young ruler thought heaven was just a payment away. It only made sense. You work hard, you pay your dues, and "zap"—your account is credited as paid in full. Jesus says, "No way." What you want costs far more than what you can pay. You don't need a system, you need a Savior. You don't need a resume, you need a Redeemer. For "what is impossible with men is possible with God."

MAX LUCADO

You shall love your neighbor as yourself.

GALATIANS 5:14, NKJV

Jesus went to great pains to be as human as the guy down the street. He didn't need to study, but still went to the synagogue. He had no need for income, but still worked in the workshop. . . . And upon his shoulders rested the challenge of redeeming creation, but he still took time to walk ninety miles from Jericho to Cana to go to a wedding.

As a result, people liked him.

I expect and hope . . . to show the greatness
of Christ in my life here on earth, whether I live or die.
PHILIPPIANS 1:20

*I*t would have been nice if God had let us order life like we order a meal. I'll take good health and a high IQ. I'll pass on the music skills, but give me a fast metabolism. . . . Would've been nice. But it didn't happen. When it came to your life on earth, you weren't given a voice or a vote.

But when it comes to life after death, you were. In my book that seems like a good deal. Wouldn't you agree?

In the beginning God created the heavens and the earth.

GENESIS 1:1, NKJV

Of all we don't know about the creation, there is one thing we do know—God did it with a smile. He must've had a blast. Painting the stripes on the zebra, hanging the stars in the sky, putting the gold in the sunset. What creativity! . . .

Like a whistling carpenter in his workshop, he loved every bit of it. He poured himself into the work. So intent was his creativity that he took a day off at the end of the week just to rest.

Love . . . does not rejoice in unrighteousness,
but rejoices with the truth.

1 CORINTHIANS 13:6, NASB

*I*sn't it good to know that even when we don't love with a perfect love, God does? He always nourishes what is right. He always applauds what is right. He has never done wrong, led one person to do wrong, or rejoiced when anyone did wrong. For he is love, and love "does not rejoice in unrighteousness, but rejoices with the truth."

MAX LUCADO

*Your faith makes you offer
your lives as a sacrifice in serving God.*

PHILIPPIANS 2:17

When we face struggles, we often wonder, *Why?* Years from now, though, we may realize that it was those struggles that taught us something we could not have otherwise learned—that there was a purpose in our pain.

God's purpose is greater than your pain, and he has a greater purpose than your problems.

You cannot add any time to your life by worrying about it.

MATTHEW 6:27

Anxiety is an expensive habit. Of course, it might be worth the cost if it worked. But it doesn't. Our frets are futile.

Worry has never brightened a day, solved a problem, or cured a disease.

God leads us. God will do the right thing at the right time. And what a difference that makes.

MAX LUCADO

You, LORD, give true peace to those who depend on you.

ISAIAH 26:3

*H*ave you got God figured out? If so,
then listen. . . .

Hear the rocks meant for the body of the
adulterous woman drop to the ground. . . .

Listen to the window from Nain eating
dinner with her son who is supposed to
be dead. . . .

God . . . doing the strangest of things.
Stretching smiles where there had
hung only frowns. Placing twinkles
where there were only tears.

Don't worry about tomorrow,
because tomorrow will have its own worries.

MATTHEW 6:34

God liberated his children from slavery and created a path through the sea. He gave them a cloud to follow in the day and a fire to see at night. And he gave them food. . . .

Each morning the manna came. Each evening the quail appeared. "Trust me. Trust me and I will give you what you need." The people were told to take just enough for one day. Their needs would be met, one day at a time.

MAX LUCADO

Receive the kingdom God has
prepared for you since the world was made.

MATTHEW 25:34

*T*he problem with this world is that it
doesn't fit. Oh, it will do for now, but it isn't
tailor-made. We were made to live with God,
but on earth we live by faith. We were made to
live forever, but on this earth we live but for a
moment. We were made to live holy lives,
but this world is stained by sin.

This world wears like a borrowed
shirt. Heaven will fit like
one tailor-made.

I will also give to each one who wins the
victory a white stone with a new name written on it.

REVELATION 2:17

You may not have known it, but God has a
new name for you. When you get home,
he won't call you Alice or Bob or Juan or
Geraldo. The name you've always heard won't
be the one he uses. When God says he will
make all things new, he means it. You will
have a new home, a new body, a new life,
and you guessed it, a new name.

MAX LUCADO

GOD's business is putting things right.

PSALM 11:7, THE MESSAGE

We don't see Jesus settling many disputes or negotiating conflicts. But we *do* see him cultivating inward harmony through acts of love:

> washing the feet of men he knew would betray him, . . .
> honoring the sinful woman whom society had scorned.

He built bridges by healing hurts.

God is so great, greater than we can understand!

JOB 36:26

We may search out the moment the first wave slapped on a shore or the first star burst in the sky, but we'll never find the first moment when God was God, for there is no moment when God was not God. He has never *not been,* for He is eternal. God is not bound by time.

When the Spirit of truth comes, he will lead you into all truth.

JOHN 16:13

Envision a father helping his son learn
to ride a bicycle, and you will have a partial
picture of the Holy Spirit. The father stays at
the son's side. He pushes the bike and steadies
it if the boy starts to tumble. The Spirit does
that for us; he stays our step and strengthens
our stride. Unlike the father, however,
he never leaves. He is with us to the end
of the age.

This is love: not that we loved God, but that
he loved us and sent his Son as an atoning sacrifice for our sins.

1 John 4:10, NIV

Does God love us because of our goodness?
Because of our kindness? Because of our
great faith? No, he loves us because of his
goodness, kindness, and great faith. John says
it like this: "This is love: not that we loved
God, but that he loved us."

Max Lucado

Every perfect gift is from God.

JAMES 1:17

An itinerant preacher from Nazareth can do something for the hurt that is in your heart. Maybe you're trying to rebuild an estranged relationship. . . . Maybe you've been trying to find God for longer than you can remember. There was something about this Nazarene preacher that made people cluster around him like he was God's gift to humanity. He is your gift as well.

I am with you always, even to the end of the age.

MATTHEW 28:20, NKJV

A storm on the Sea of Galilee was akin to a sumo wrestler's belly flop on a kiddy pool. The northern valley acted like a wind tunnel, compressing and hosing squalls onto the lake. Waves as tall as ten feet were common. . . .

[Yet] from the center of the storm, the unwavering Jesus shouts, "I am." Tall in the Trade Tower wreckage. Bold against the Galilean waves. ICU, battlefield, boardroom, prison cell, or maternity ward—whatever your storm, "I am."

MAX LUCADO

*When you hurt,
God hurts with you.*

Human life comes from human parents,
but spiritual life comes from the Spirit.

JOHN 3:6

*S*piritual life comes from the Spirit!
Your parents may have given you genes, but
God gives you grace. Your parents may be
responsible for your body, but God has taken
charge of your soul. You may get your looks
from your mother, but you get eternity from
your Father, your heavenly Father.

MAX LUCADO

You did not choose me; I chose you.

JOHN 15:16

If you ever wonder how God can use you to make a difference in your world, just look at those he has already used and take heart. Look at the forgiveness found in his open arms and take courage.

And, by the way, never were those arms opened so wide as they were on the Roman cross. One arm extending back into history and the other reaching into the future. An embrace of forgiveness offered for anyone who'll come.

The kingdom of heaven is like a treasure hidden in a field.

MATTHEW 13:44

When you list the places Christ lived, draw a circle around the town named Nazareth—a single-camel map dot on the edge of boredom. For thirty of his thirty-three years, Jesus lived a common life. . . .

And the town may have been common, but his attention to it was not. . . . He saw how a seed on the path took no root (Luke 8:5) and how a mustard seed produced a great tree (Matt. 13:31–32). Jesus listened to his common life.

Are you listening to yours?

MAX LUCADO

His love has taken over our lives;
God's faithful ways are eternal.

PSALM 117:2, THE MESSAGE

God's love for you is not dependent on how you look, how you think, how you act, or how perfect you are. His love is absolutely nonnegotiable and nonreturnable. Ours is a faithful God.

Anyone who is having troubles should pray.

JAMES 5:13

*H*ave you taken your disappointments to God? You've shared them with your neighbor, your relatives, your friends. But have you taken them to God?

Before you go anywhere else with your disappointments, go to God.

MAX LUCADO

Let anyone who is thirsty come to me and drink.

JOHN 7:37

God is a God who opens the door and waves His hand, pointing pilgrims to a full table.

His invitation is not just for a meal, however. It is for life. An invitation to come into His kingdom and take up residence in a tearless, graveless, painless world. Who can come? Whoever wishes. The invitation is at once universal and personal.

"Master, how many times do I
forgive a brother or sister who hurts me? Seven?"
MATTHEW 18:21, THE MESSAGE

*T*he Jewish law stipulated that the wounded forgive three times. Peter is willing to double that and throw in one more for good measure. No doubt he thinks Jesus will be impressed. Jesus isn't. The Master's answer still stuns us. "Seven! Hardly. Try seventy times seven" (v. 22, THE MESSAGE).

If you're pausing to multiply seventy times seven, you're missing the point. Keeping tabs on your mercy, Jesus is saying, is not being merciful.

MAX LUCADO

Don't let your hearts be troubled. Trust in God, and trust in me.

JOHN 14:1

Don't be troubled by the return of Christ. Don't be anxious about things you cannot comprehend. Issues like the millennium and the Antichrist are intended to challenge and stretch us, but not overwhelm and certainly not divide us. For the Christian, the return of Christ is not a riddle to be solved or a code to be broken, but rather a day to be anticipated.

Jesus wants us to trust him.

Thine is the kingdom and the power and the glory forever.
MATTHEW 6:13, RSV

"Thine is the kingdom and the power and the glory forever." What protection this . . . phrase affords. As you confess that God is in charge, you admit that you aren't. As you proclaim that God has power, you admit that you don't. And as you give God all the applause, there is none left to dizzy your brain.

MAX LUCADO

Blessed are those who mourn, for they shall be comforted.

MATTHEW 5:4, NKJV

To mourn for your sins is a natural outflow of poverty of spirit. . . . Many know they are wrong, yet pretend they are right. As a result, they never taste the exquisite sorrow of repentance.

Of all the paths to joy, this one has to be the strangest. True blessedness, Jesus says, begins with deep sadness.

Be agreeable, be sympathetic,
be loving, be compassionate, be humble.

1   P E T E R   3 : 8 ,   T H E   M E S S A G E

*T*hey called Jesus a blasphemer, but they never called him a braggart. They accused him of heresy, but never arrogance. He was branded as a radical, but never unapproachable.

There is no hint that he ever used his heavenly status for personal gain. Ever. You just don't get the impression that his neighbors grew sick of his haughtiness and asked, "Well, who do you think made you God?"

His faith made him likable.

M A X   L U C A D O

This is my commitment to my people: removal of their sins.

ROMANS 11:27, THE MESSAGE

God does more than forgive our mistakes; he removes them! We simply have to take them to him.

He not only wants the mistakes we've made. He wants the ones we are making. Are you making some? . . .

If so, don't pretend nothing is wrong. . . . Go first to God. The first step after a stumble must be in the direction of the cross.

In the past God spoke . . . at many times and in various ways,
but in these last days he has spoken to us by his Son.

HEBREWS 1:1–2, NIV

God, motivated by love and directed by divinity, surprised everyone. He became a man. In an untouchable mystery, he disguised himself as a carpenter and lived in a dusty Judean village. Determined to prove his love for his creation, he walked incognito through his own world. His calloused hands touched wounds and his compassionate words touched hearts. He became one of us.

MAX LUCADO

Love . . . bears all things, believes all things,
hopes all things, endures all things.

1 CORINTHIANS 13:4−7, NKJV

The apostle is looking for a ribbon to wrap around one of the sweetest paragraphs in Scripture. I envision the leathery-faced saint pausing in his dictation. . . . Checking off his fingers, he reviews his list. "Let's see, patience, kindness, envy, arrogance. We've mentioned rudeness, selfishness, and anger, forgiveness, evil, and truth. Have I covered all things? Ah, that's it—all things. Here, write this down. Love bears all things, believes all things, hopes all things, endures all things."

The moment I called out, you stepped in;
you made my life large with strength.

PSALM 138:3, THE MESSAGE

Where is God when we hurt? Where is he when sleep won't come? Where is he when we awaken in a hospital bed with pain that won't subside? He's right here! He hung on the gallows to prove once and for all, with pierced hands and blood-stained face—that he's here—that he didn't create the hurt, but he came to take it away.

When you hurt, God hurts with you.

God is greater than our hearts, and he knows everything.

1 JOHN 3:20

You and I are governed. The weather determines what we wear. The terrain tells us how to travel. . . .

God—our Shepherd—doesn't check the weather; He makes it. He doesn't defy gravity; He created it.

God is what He is. What He has always been. God is Yahweh—an unchanging God, an uncaused God, and an ungoverned God.

Man . . . heaps up wealth, not knowing who will get it.

PSALM 39:6, NIV

We need one day in which work comes to a screeching halt. We need one twenty-four hour period in which the wheels stop grinding and the motor stops turning. We need to stop. . . .

Slow down. If God commanded it, you need it. If Jesus modeled it, you need it. . . . Take a day to say no to work and yes to worship.

MAX LUCADO

The Son gives life.

JOHN 5:21

The Bible is the story of two gardens: Eden and Gethsemane. In the first, Adam took a fall. In the second, Jesus took a stand. In the first, God sought Adam. In the second, Jesus sought God. In Eden, Adam hid from God. In Gethsemane, Jesus emerged from the tomb. In Eden, Satan led Adam to a tree that led to his death. From Gethsemane, Jesus went to a tree that led to our life.

*"The lad and I will go yonder
and worship, and we will come back to you."*

GENESIS 22:5, NKJV

braham is about to sacrifice his only son—
and what word does he use to describe the act?
"Worship." He's headed up the mountain to
place the biggest part of his life on an altar
and he calls it "Worship."

When we think of worship we typically
think of offering a song, or a prayer, or a
gift. But when Abraham worshiped, he offered
his son. He offered the biggest part of his life
to God.

The blind receive sight, the lame walk,
those who have leprosy are cured, the deaf hear.

MATTHEW 11:5, NIV

None were more shunned by their culture than the blind, the lame, the lepers, and the deaf. They had no place. No name. No value. Canker sores on the culture. Excess baggage on the side of the road. But those whom the people called trash, Jesus called treasures.

Jesus took the loaves of bread,
thanked God for them, and gave them to the people.

JOHN 6:11

When the disciples didn't pray, Jesus prayed. When the disciples didn't see God, Jesus sought God. When the disciples were weak, Jesus was strong. When the disciples had no faith, Jesus had faith. He thanked God. . . .

God is faithful even when his children are not.

That's what makes God, God.

MAX LUCADO

The Spirit produces the fruit of love, joy, peace, patience,
kindness, goodness, faithfulness, gentleness, self-control.

GALATIANS 5:22

*L*ove is a fruit. A fruit of whom? Of your
hard work? Of your deep faith? Of your
rigorous resolve? No. Love is a fruit of the
Spirit of God. "The Spirit *produces* the fruit
of love" (Gal. 5:22, NCV, italics added).

God sent his Son . . . so we could become his children.

GALATIANS 4:4–5

W e . . . were orphans.

Alone.

No name. No future. No hope.

Were it not for our adoption as God's children we would have no place to belong. We sometimes forget that.

MAX LUCADO

Set your mind on the things above,
not on the things that are on earth.

COLOSSIANS 3:2, NASB

As Christ dominates your thoughts,
he changes you from one degree of glory to
another until—hang on!—you are ready to live
with him.

Heaven is the land of sinless minds. . . .
Absolute trust. No fear or anger. . . . Heaven
will be wonderful, not because the streets are
gold, but because our thoughts will be pure.

We do not know how to pray as we should.
But the Spirit himself speaks to God for us.

ROMANS 8:26

You know, we really don't know what to pray for, do we? What if God had answered every prayer that you ever prayed? Just think who you'd be married to. Just think where you'd be living. Just think what you'd be doing.

God loves us so much that sometimes he gives us what we need and not what we ask.

MAX LUCADO

*All people will know that you
are my followers if you love each other.*

JOHN 13:35

*S*top and think about that verse for a
minute. Could it be that unity is the key to
reaching the world for Christ? . . .

Nowhere, by the way, are we told to
build unity. We are told simply to *keep* unity.
From God's perspective there is but "one
flock and one shepherd" (John 10:16).
Unity does not need to be created; it simply
needs to be protected.

The Word became flesh and dwelt among us.

JOHN 1:14, NKJV

*J*esus was touchable, approachable, reachable. . . .

He was the kind of fellow you'd invite to watch the Rams-Giants game at your house. He'd wrestle on the floor with your kids, doze on your couch, and cook steaks on your grill. He'd laugh at your jokes and tell a few of his own. And when you spoke, he'd listen to you as if he had all the time in eternity.

And one thing's for sure, you'd invite him back.

*Let your light shine before men, that they may
see your good deeds and praise your Father in heaven.*

MATTHEW 5:16, NIV

*D*id you notice the first five letters of the
word *courteous* spell *court?* In old England,
to be courteous was to act in the way of the
court. The family and servants of the king
were expected to follow a higher standard.

So are we. Are we not called to represent
the King? Then "let your light shine before
men, that they may see your good deeds and
praise your Father in heaven."

MARCH

Kind hearts
are quietly kind.

With one sacrifice he made perfect
forever those who are being made holy.

HEBREWS 10:14

*U*nderline the word *perfect*. Note that the word is not *better*. Not *improving*. Not *on the upswing*. God doesn't improve; he perfects. He doesn't enhance; he completes. . . .

When he sees each of us, he sees one who has been made perfect through the One who is perfect—Jesus Christ.

*A crown is being held for . . . all those
who have waited with love for him to come again.*

2 TIMOTHY 4:8

We understand that in the economy of
earth, there are a limited number of crowns.

The economy of heaven, however, is
refreshingly different. Heavenly rewards are
not limited to a chosen few, but "to all those
who have waited with love for him to come
again." The three-letter word *all* is a gem.
The winner's circle isn't reserved for a
handful of the elite but
for a heaven full of
God's children.

*The law of the Spirit that brings life
made me free from the law that brings sin and death.*

ROMANS 8:3

*T*he cross did what sacrificed lambs could not do. It erased our sins, not for a year, but for eternity. The cross did what man could not do. It granted us the right to talk with, love, and even live with God.

You can't do that by yourself. I don't care how many worship services you attend or good deeds you do, your goodness is insufficient. . . . That's why we need a savior.

He who began a good work in you will carry
it on to completion until the day of Christ Jesus.

PHILIPPIANS 1:6, NIV

*R*eligious rule-keeping can sap your
strength. It's endless. There is always another
class to attend, Sabbath to obey, Ramadan to
observe. No prison is as endless as the prison
of perfection. Her inmates find work but
never find peace. How could they? They never
know when they are finished.

Christ . . . fulfilled the law for you.
Bid farewell to the burden of religion. . . .
God pledges to help those who stop trying
to help themselves.

When I see the blood, I will pass over you.

EXODUS 12:13

*T*he blood on the doorpost reminds us . . .
that it wasn't Moses who set the Hebrews free.
It was God. The blood on the doorpost
reminds us of blood smeared on another post.
Blood of another lamb.
The Lamb of God.
Because of his blood, we, too, are free.

MAX LUCADO

*The LORD is God. He made us, and we
belong to him; we are his people, the sheep he tends.*

PSALM 100:3

Sheep aren't the only ones who need a
healing touch. We also get irritated with each
other, butt heads, and then get wounded.
Many of our disappointments in life begin as
irritations. The large portion of our problems
is not lion-sized attacks, but rather the day-
to-day swarm of frustrations and mishaps
and heartaches.

"I will be a Father to you, and you shall be
My sons and daughters," says the LORD Almighty.

2 CORINTHIANS 6:18, NKJV

God did what we wouldn't dare dream.
He did what we couldn't imagine. He became
a man so we could trust Him. He became a
sacrifice so we could know Him. And He
defeated death so we could follow Him. . . .

Only a Creator beyond the fence of logic
could offer such a gift of love.

MAX LUCADO

There is now no condemnation
for those who are in Jesus Christ.

ROMANS 8:1, NIV

There is never a point at which you are any less saved than you were the first moment Christ saved you. Just because you were grumpy at breakfast doesn't mean you were condemned at breakfast. When you lost your temper yesterday, you didn't lose your salvation. Your name doesn't disappear and reappear in the book of life according to your moods and actions. . . .

You are saved, not because of what you do, but because of what Christ did.

They knew nothing about what was happening
until the flood came and destroyed them. It will be the same
when the Son of Man comes.

MATTHEW 24:39

Noah was sent to save the faithful.
Christ was sent to do the same. A flood of
water came then. A flood of fire will come
next. Noah built a safe place out of wood.
Jesus made a safe place with the cross.
Those who believed hid in the ark. Those
who believe are hidden in Christ.

MAX LUCADO

Gideon built an altar . . . and named it The LORD Is Peace.

JUDGES 6:24

"Y-y-you b-b-better get somebody else," we stammer. But then God reminds us that he knows we can't, but he can, and to prove it he gives a wonderful gift. He brings a spirit of peace. A peace before the storm. A peace beyond logic. . . . He gave it to David after he showed him Goliath; he gave it to Saul after he showed him the gospel; he gave it to Jesus after he showed him the cross.

Guide me in your truth, and teach me, my God, my Savior.

PSALM 25:5

"It's not fair," we say. It's not fair that I was born in poverty or that I sing so poorly or that I run so slowly. But the scales of life were forever tipped on the side of fairness when God planted a tree in the Garden of Eden. All complaints were silenced when Adam and his descendants were given free will, the freedom to make whatever eternal choice we desire. Any injustice in this life is offset by the honor of choosing our destiny in the next.

MAX LUCADO

The greatest love a person can show is to die for his friends.

JOHN 15:13

I like John most for the way he loved Jesus. His relationship with Jesus was, . . . simple. To John, Jesus was a good friend with a good heart and a good idea. . . .

One gets the impression that to John, Jesus was above all a loyal companion. Messiah? Yes. Son of God? Indeed. Miracle worker? That, too. But more than anything . . . Jesus was a friend.

You did not save yourselves; it was a gift from God.

EPHESIANS 2:8

We hide. He seeks. We bring sin. He brings a sacrifice. We try fig leaves. He brings the robe of righteousness. And we are left to sing the song of the prophet: "He has covered me with clothes of salvation and wrapped me with a coat of goodness, like a bridegroom dressed for his wedding, like a bride dressed in jewels" (Isa. 61:10).

God has clothed us. He protects us with a cloak of love.

There will be no more death, sadness,
crying, or pain, because all the old ways are gone.

REVELATION 21:4

*F*olks, if you're expecting to be given a fair
shake in your life, forget it! You won't be.
You're going to face illness. And your body is
going to wear out. You may be the victim of
someone else's mistake. But you can get
through those tough times if you prepare you
heart now, living to know and serve
the Savior who loves you
and died so that you might
have an eternal home
free of pain and sorrow.

He rested on the seventh day.

EXODUS 20:11, THE MESSAGE

Read what Jesus did during the last Sabbath of his life. Start in the Gospel of Matthew. Didn't find anything? Try Mark. . . . Nothing there either? Strange. What about Luke? . . . Not a word about it? Well, try John. Surely John mentions the Sabbath. He doesn't? No reference? Hmmmm. Looks like Jesus was quiet that day. . . .

"You mean with one week left to live, Jesus observed the Sabbath?" As far as we can tell.

MAX LUCADO

Your love, GOD, is my song, and I'll sing it!
PSALM 89:1, THE MESSAGE

God's love is not human. His love is not normal. His love sees your sin and loves you still. Does he approve of your error? No. Do you need to repent? Yes. But do you repent for his sake or yours? Yours. His ego needs no apology. His love needs no bolstering.

And he could not love you more than he does right now.

I pray that you and all God's holy people will have
the power to understand the greatness of Christ's love.

EPHESIANS 3:18

From the cradle in Bethlehem to the cross in Jerusalem we've pondered the love of our Father. What can you say to that kind of emotion? Upon learning that God would rather die than live without you, how do you react? How can you begin to explain such passion?

If people say they have faith, but do nothing,
their faith is worth nothing. Can faith like that save them?

James' message is bare-knuckled; his style is bare-boned. Talk is cheap, he argues. Service is invaluable.

It's not that works save the Christian, but that works mark the Christian. In James' book of logic, it only makes sense that we who have been given much should give much. Not just with words. But with our lives.

When I am afraid, I put my trust in you.

PSALM 56:3, NLT

*H*ow did Jesus endure the terror of the crucifixion? He went first to the Father with his fears.

Do the same with yours. Don't avoid life's Gardens of Gethsemane. Enter them. Just don't enter them alone. And while there, be honest. Pounding the ground is permitted. Tears are allowed. . . .

And be specific. . . . He knows what you need.

MAX LUCADO

The person who is forgiven only a little will love only a little.

LUKE 7:47

To believe we are totally and eternally debt free is seldom easy. Even if we've stood before the throne and heard it from the king himself, we still doubt. As a result, many are forgiven only a little, not because the grace of the king is limited, but because the faith of the sinner is small. God is willing to forgive all. He's willing to wipe the slate completely clean. He guides us to a pool of mercy and invites us to bathe. Some plunge in, but others just touch the surface.

He poured out His soul unto death.

ISAIAH 53:12, NKJV

*T*he scene is very simple; you'll recognize it quickly. A grove of twisted olive trees. Ground cluttered with large rocks. A low stone fence. A dark, dark night. . . .

See that solitary figure? . . . Flat on the ground. Face stained with dirt and tears. Fists pounding the hard earth. . . .

That's Jesus. . . . God was never more human than at this hour. God was never nearer to us than when he hurt.

*This man was handed over to you
by God's set purpose and foreknowledge.*

ACTS 2:23, NIV

*J*esus planned his own sacrifice.

He intentionally planted the tree from which his cross would be carved.

He willingly placed the iron ore in the heart of earth from which the nails would be cast. . . .

Christ was the one who set in motion the political machinery that would send Pilate to Jerusalem. . . .

He didn't have to do it—but he did.

When we have the opportunity to help anyone, we should do it.
GALATIANS 6:10

Kind hearts are quietly kind. They let the car cut into traffic and the young mom with three kids move up in the checkout line. They pick up the neighbor's trash can that rolled into the street. And they are especially kind at church. They understand that perhaps the neediest person they'll meet all week is the one standing in the foyer or sitting on the row behind them in worship.

MAX LUCADO

The Good Shepherd puts the sheep before himself.

JOHN 10:11, THE MESSAGE

God is on a cross. The creator of the
universe is being executed.

Spit and blood are caked to his cheeks,
and his lips are cracked and swollen.
Thorns rip his scalp. His lungs scream with
pain. His legs knot with cramps. . . .
And there is no one to save him, for he is
sacrificing himself.

It is no normal six hours . . . it is
no normal Friday.

By Him all things were created, both in
the heavens and on earth, visible and invisible, whether thrones
or dominions or rulers or authorities.

COLOSSIANS 1:16, NASB

What a phenomenal list! Heavens and earth. Visible and invisible. Thrones, dominions, rulers, and authorities. No thing, place, or person omitted. The scale on the sea urchin. The hair on the elephant hide. The hurricane that wrecks the coast, the rain that nourishes the desert, the infant's first heartbeat, the elderly person's final breath—all can be traced back to the hand of Christ, the firstborn of creation.

MAX LUCADO

The LORD won't leave his people nor give up his children.

PSALM 94:14

When everyone else rejects you, Christ accepts you. When everyone else leaves you, Christ finds you. When no one else wants you, Christ claims you. When no one else will give you the time of day, Jesus will give you the words of eternity. . . .

What is the work of God? Accepting people. . . . Caring before condemning.

At noon the whole country was covered
with darkness, which lasted for three hours.

MATTHEW 27:45, TEV

Of course the sky is dark; people are killing the Light of the World. . . .

The sky weeps. And a lamb bleats. Remember the time of the scream? "At about three o'clock Jesus cried out." Three o'clock in the afternoon, the hour of the temple sacrifice. Less than a mile to the east, a finely clothed priest leads a lamb to the slaughter, unaware that his work is futile. Heaven is not looking at the lamb of man but at "the Lamb of God, who takes away the sin of the world" (John 1:29, RSV).

God is strong and can help you not to fall.

JUDE 24

Can God really keep you from falling? To answer that, go to a . . . tree on a barren hill. A tree older than time. A tree that covers the mistakes of your past and the problems of your future. Be assured—that tree will never fall.

"Father, forgive them, for they do not know what they are doing."

LUKE 23:34, NIV

*H*ow Jesus, with a body wracked with pain, eyes blinded by his own blood, and lungs yearning for air, could speak on behalf of some heartless thugs is beyond my comprehension. Never, never have I seen such love. If ever a person deserved a shot at revenge, Jesus did. But he didn't take it. Instead he died for them. How could he do it? I don't know. But I do know that all of a sudden my wounds seem very painless. My grudges and hard feelings are suddenly childish.

*He himself is our peace . . . and has
destroyed the barrier, the dividing wall of hostility.*

EPHESIANS 2:14, NIV

We are guilty and He is innocent.

We are filthy and He is pure.

We are wrong and He is right.

He is not on that cross for His sins. He is
there for ours.

"This man has done nothing wrong."

LUKE 23:41

*F*inally someone is defending Jesus. Peter fled. The disciples hid. The Jews accused. Pilate washed his hands. Many could have spoken on behalf of Jesus, but none did. Until now. Kind words from the lips of a thief. He makes his request. "Jesus, remember me when you come into your kingdom" (Luke 23:42).

The Savior turns his heavy head toward the prodigal child and promises, "Today you will be with me in paradise" (Luke 23:43).

MAX LUCADO

APRIL

God never gives up.

I have said these things to you that my joy may be in you.

JOHN 15:11, RSV

Think about God's joy. What can cloud it? What can quench it? . . . Is God ever in a bad mood because of bad weather? Does God get ruffled over long lines or traffic jams? Does God ever refuse to rotate the earth because his feelings are hurt?

No. His is a joy which consequences cannot quench. His is a peace which circumstances cannot steal.

MAX LUCADO

He had no special beauty or form to make us notice him.

ISAIAH 53:2

*D*rop-dead smile? Steal-your-breath physique? No. Heads didn't turn when Jesus passed. If he was anything like his peers, he had a broad peasant's face, dark olive skin, short curly hair, and a prominent nose. He stood five feet one inch tall and weighed around 110 pounds. Hardly worthy of a *GQ* cover. . . .

Are your looks run-of-the-mill and your ways simple? So were his. He's been there.

There are many rooms in my Father's house;
I would not tell you this if it were not true.

JOHN 14:2

"It is finished!" he cried.

And the great Creator went home.

(He's not resting though. Word has it that his tireless hands are preparing a city so glorious even the angels get goose bumps upon seeing it. Considering what he has done so far, that is one creation I plan to see.)

MAX LUCADO

If the Son makes you free, you will be truly free.

JOHN 8:36

Trying to make it to heaven on our own goodness is like trying to get to the moon on a moon beam; nice idea, but try it and see what happens.

Listen. Quit trying to quench your own guilt. You can't do it. There's no way. Not with a bottle of whiskey or perfect Sunday school attendance. Sorry. I don't care how bad you are. You can't be bad enough to forget it. And I don't care how good you are. You can't be good enough to overcome it. You need a Savior.

The Spirit produces the fruit of love, joy, peace, patience.

GALATIANS 5:22

Have you asked God to give you some fruit? *Well I did once, but . . .* But what? Did you, h'm, grow impatient? Ask him again and again and again. He won't grow impatient with your pleading, and you will receive patience in your praying.

And while you're praying, ask for understanding. "Patient people have great understanding" (Prov. 14:29). Could it be your impatience stems from a lack of understanding? Mine has.

MAX LUCADO

We are completely free to enter the Most Holy Place. . . .
We can enter through . . . the curtain—Christ's body.

HEBREWS 10:19–20

*T*o the original readers, those last four words were explosive: "the curtain—Christ's body." According to the writer, the curtain equals Jesus. Hence, whatever happened to the flesh of Jesus happened to the curtain. What happened to his flesh? It was torn. Torn by the whips, torn by the thorns. Torn by the weight of the cross and the point of the nails. But in the horror of his torn flesh, we find the splendor of the open door. . . . We are welcome to enter into God's presence— any day, any time.

No one can enter the Kingdom of God
without being born of water and the Spirit.
JOHN 3:5, NLT

When you believe in Christ, Christ works a miracle in you. "When you believed in Christ, he identified you as his own by giving you the Holy Spirit" (Eph. 1:13, NLT). You are permanently purified and empowered by God himself. The message of Jesus to the religious person is simple: It's not what you do. It's what I do. I have moved in. And in time you can say with Paul, "I myself no longer live, but Christ lives in me" (Gal. 2:20, NLT).

Nothing above us, nothing below us,
nor anything else in the whole world will ever be able to separate
us from the love of God that is in Christ Jesus.

ROMANS 8:39

No matter what you do, no matter how far you fall, no matter how ugly you become, God has a relentless, undying, unfathomable, unquenchable love from which you cannot be separated. Ever!

"Surely this was a righteous man."
LUKE 23:47, NIV

All the Roman centurion did was see Jesus suffer. He never heard him preach or saw him heal or followed him through the crowds. He never witnessed him still the wind; he only witnessed the way he died. But that was all it took to cause this weather-worn soldier to take a giant step in faith. "Surely this was a righteous man." . . .

Anybody can preach a sermon on a mount surrounded by daisies. But only one with a gut full of faith can *live* a sermon on a mountain of pain.

God will always give what is right to his people who cry to him night and day, and he will not be slow to answer them.

LUKE 18:7

When we come to God, we make requests; we don't make demands. We come with high hopes and a humble heart. We state what we want, but we pray for what is right. And if God gives us the prison of Rome instead of the mission of Spain, we accept it because we know *"God will always give what is right to his people."*

We go to him. We bow before him, and *we trust in him.*

Those people who keep their faith until the end will be saved.

MATTHEW 24:13

*I*n Portuguese, a person who has the ability to hang in and not give up has *garra*. *Garra* means *"claws."* What imagery! A person with *garra* has claws which burrow in the side of the cliff and keep him from falling.

So do the saved. They may get close to the edge, they may even stumble and slide.

But they will dig their nails into the rock of God and hang on.

MAX LUCADO

He isn't here! He has been raised from the dead.

MATTHEW 28:6, NLT

The crucifixion was marked by sudden darkness, silent angels, and mocking soldiers. At the empty tomb the soldiers are silent, an angel speaks, and light erupts like Vesuvius. The one who was dead is said to be alive, and the soldiers, who are alive, look as if they are dead. The women can tell something is up. . . . The angel informs them: "He isn't here! He has been raised from the dead." . . .

Heaven unplugged the grave's power cord, and you and I have nothing to fear. Death is disabled.

God began doing a good work in you,
and I am sure he will continue it until it is finished.

PHILIPPIANS 1:6

Not only are we ignorant about yesterday, we are ignorant about tomorrow. Dare we judge a book while chapters are yet unwritten? . . . How can you dismiss a soul until God's work is complete?

Be careful! The Peter who denies Jesus at tonight's fire may proclaim him with fire at tomorrow's Pentecost. . . . A stammering shepherd in this generation may be the mighty Moses of the next.

MAX LUCADO

There are many rooms in my Father's house.

JOHN 14:2

*J*esus goes from heart to heart, asking if he might enter. . . .

Every so often, he is welcomed. Someone throws open the door of his or her heart and invites him to stay. And to that person Jesus gives this great promise: " . . . In my Father's house are many rooms."

"I have ample space for you," he says. . . . We make room for him in our hearts, and he makes room for us in his house.

Christ died for our sins.

1 CORINTHIANS 15:3

*T*he cross. . . .

My, what a piece of wood! History has idolized it and despised it, gold-plated it and burned it, worn and trashed it. History has done everything to it but ignore it.

That's the one option the cross does not offer.

No one can ignore it!

MAX LUCADO

His unchanging plan has always been to adopt us into his own family by sending Jesus Christ to die for us.

EPHESIANS 1:3, TLB

And you thought God adopted you because you were good-looking. You thought he needed your money or your wisdom. Sorry. God adopted you simply because he wanted to. You were in his good will and pleasure. Knowing full well the trouble you would be and the price he would pay, he signed his name next to yours and changed your name to his and took you home. Your *Abba* adopted you and became your Father.

"Go, tell his disciples and Peter
that he is going before you to Galilee."

MARK 16:7, NIV

*I*f I might paraphrase the words, "Don't stay here, go tell the disciples," a pause, then a smile, "and especially tell Peter, that he is going before you to Galilee." . . .

It's as if all of heaven had watched Peter fall—and it's as if all of heaven wanted to help him back up again. . . . No wonder they call it the gospel of the second chance.

MAX LUCADO

*When Moses reached out and took hold
of the snake, it again became a stick in his hand.*

EXODUS 4:4

*J*ust as Moses' hand touched the squirmy scales of the snake, it hardened. And Moses lifted up the rod. . . . The same rod he would lift up to divide the water and guide two million people through a desert. The rod that would remind Moses that if God can make a stick become a snake, then become a stick again—then perhaps he can do something with stubborn hearts and a stiff-necked people.

Perhaps he can do something with the common.

I identified myself completely with him. . . .
I have been crucified with Christ.

GALATIANS 2:19, THE MESSAGE

For every cunning Caiaphas there was a daring Nicodemus. For every cynical Herod there was a questioning Pilate. . . . For every turncoat Judas there was a faithful John. There was something about the crucifixion that made every witness either step toward it or away from it. . . .

Two thousand years later, the same is true. . . . We can do what we want with the cross. We can examine its history. We can study its theology. . . . Yet the one thing we can't do is walk away neutral.

MAX LUCADO

What a wonderful God we have . . .
who so wonderfully comforts and strengthens us.

2 CORINTHIANS 1:3, TLB

*E*ncourage those who are struggling. Don't know what to say? Then open your Bible. . . .

To the grief stricken: "God has said, 'Never will I leave you; never will I forsake you'" (Heb. 13:5 NIV).

To the guilt ridden: "There is now no condemnation for those who are in Christ Jesus" (Rom. 8:1 NIV).

Thomas said, "I will not believe it until I see the
nail marks in his hands and put my finger where the nails were."
JOHN 20:25

*J*esus . . . gave Thomas exactly what he
requested. He extended his hands one more
time. And was Thomas ever surprised. He did
a double take, fell flat in his face, and cried,
"My Lord and my God!" (John 20:28)

Jesus must have smiled. He knew he had
a winner in Thomas. . . . Legend has him
hopping a freighter to India where they had to
kill him to get him to quit talking about his . . .
friend who came back from the dead.

I am the good shepherd. I know
my sheep. . . . and my sheep know me.

JOHN 10:14-15

*Y*ou have a God who hears you, the power of
love behind you, the Holy Spirit within you,
and all of heaven ahead of you. If you have
the Shepherd, you have grace for every sin,
direction for every turn, a candle for every
corner, and an anchor for every storm.
You have everything you need.

All of us became part of Christ when we were baptized.

ROMANS 6:3

We owe God a perfect life. Perfect obedience to every command. Not just the command of baptism, but the commands of humility, honesty, integrity. We can't deliver. Might as well charge us for the property of Manhattan. But Christ can and he did. His plunge into the Jordan is a picture of his plunge into our sin. His baptism announces, "Let me pay."

Your baptism responds, "You bet I will." He publicly offers. We publicly accept.

*We must pay more careful
attention, therefore, to what we have heard.*

HEBREWS 2:1, NIV

*S*tability in the storm comes not from
seeking a new message but from understanding
an old one. The most reliable anchor points
are not recent discoveries, but are time-tested
truths that have held their ground against the
winds of change. Truths like:

My life is not futile. My failures are not
fatal. My death is not final.

He gives grace to the humble.

JAMES 4:6

*H*eaven may have a shrine to honor God's uncommon use of the common.

It's a place you won't want to miss. Stroll through and see Rahab's rope, Paul's bucket, David's sling, and Samson's jawbone. Wrap your hand around the staff that split the sea and smote the rock. Sniff the ointment that soothed Jesus' skin and lifted his heart. . . .

I don't know if these items will be there. But I am sure of one thing—the people who used them will.

He went into the hills to pray.

MARK 6:46

What does Jesus do while we are in the storm? You'll love this. He prays for us. . . .

So where does that leave us? While Jesus is praying and we are in the storm, what are we to do? Simple. We do what the disciples did. We row. . . .

Much of life is spent rowing. . . . Getting out of bed. Fixing lunches. . . . More struggle than strut.

You shall receive power when the Holy Spirit has come upon you.
ACTS 1:8, NKJV

Remember the followers' fear at the crucifixion? They ran. Scared as cats in a dog pound. . . .

But fast-forward forty days. . . . Peter is preaching in the very precinct where Christ was arrested. Followers of Christ defy the enemies of Christ. . . . As bold after the Resurrection as they were cowardly before it.

Explanation? A resurrected Christ and his Holy Spirit. The courage of these men and women was forged in the fire of the empty tomb.

MAX LUCADO

He ranks higher than everything that has been made.

COLOSSIANS 1:15

*E*verything? Find an exception. Peter's mother-in-law has a fever; Jesus rebukes it. A tax needs to be paid; Jesus pays it by sending first a coin and then a fisherman's hook into the mouth of a fish. When five thousand stomachs growl, Jesus renders a boy's basket a bottomless buffet. Jesus exudes authority. He bats an eyelash, and nature jumps. No one argues when, at the end of his earthly life, the God-man declares, "All authority has been given to Me in heaven and on earth" (Matt. 28:18, NASB).

God is the strength of my heart.

PSALM 73:26, NKJV

God is for you. Turn to the sidelines;
that's God cheering your run. Look past the
finish line; that's God applauding your steps.
Listen for Him in the bleachers, shouting
your name. Too tired to continue?
He'll carry you. Too discouraged to fight?
He's picking you up. God is *for* you.

MAX LUCADO

Our Lord God, the Almighty, rules. Let us rejoice and be happy.

REVELATION 19:6–7

*I*n the Book of Revelation . . . we, the soldiers are privileged a glimpse into the final battlefield. All hell breaks loose as all heaven comes forth. The two collide in the ultimate battle of good and evil. Left standing amidst the smoke and thunder is the Son of God. Jesus, born in a manger—now triumphant over Satan. . . .

And we, the soldiers are assured of victory.

Let us march.

MAY

*We were
made to live
with God.*

He bruises, but He binds up;
He wounds, but His hands make whole.

JOB 5:18, NKJV

Oh, the hands of Jesus. Hands of incarnation at his birth. Hands of liberation as he healed. Hands of inspiration as he taught. Hands of dedication as he served. And hands of salvation as he died. . . .

The same hand that cleansed the Temple cleanses your heart.

The hand is the hand of God.

The testimony of the LORD is sure, making wise the simple.

PSALM 19:7, NKJV

"God's testimony," wrote David, "makes wise the simple."

God's testimony. When was the last time you witnessed it? A stroll through knee-high grass in a green meadow. An hour listening to seagulls or . . . witnessing the shafts of sunlight brighten the snow on a crisp winter dawn. Miracles . . . happen all around us; we only have to pay attention.

I count everything as loss because of the surpassing worth of knowing Christ Jesus my Lord.

PHILIPPIANS 3:8, RSV

*H*e was, the single most significant person who ever lived. . . . The head of the parade? Hardly. No one else shares the street. Who comes close? Humanity's best and brightest fade like dime-store rubies next to him. . . .

A just-God Jesus could make us but not understand us. A just-man Jesus could love us but never save us. But a God-man Jesus? Near enough to touch. Strong enough to trust.

When I was desperate, I called out,
and GOD got me out of a tight spot.

PSALM 34:6, THE MESSAGE

*R*un to Jesus. Jesus wants you to go to him.
He wants to become the most important
person in your life, the greatest love you'll
ever know. He wants you to love him so much
that there's no room in your heart and in
your life for sin. Invite him to take up
residence in your heart.

*If we are not faithful, he will still
be faithful, because he cannot be false to himself.*

2 TIMOTHY 2:13

Our moods may shift, but God's doesn't.
Our minds may change, but God's doesn't.
Our devotion may falter, but God's never does.
Even if we are faithless, He is faithful, for He
cannot betray himself. He is a sure God.

MAX LUCADO

The Lord himself will come down

from heaven, with a loud command.

1 THESSALONIANS 4:16, NIV

*H*ave you ever wondered what that
command will be? It will be the inaugural
word of heaven.

I could very well be wrong, but I think the
command that puts an end to the pains of
the earth and initiates the joys of heaven will
be two words: "No more."

No more loneliness. No more tears.
No more death. No more sadness.
No more crying. No more pain.

"Today you will be with me in Paradise."

LUKE 23:43

A condemned criminal was sent to his death by his country. In his final moments, he asked for mercy. Had he asked for mercy from the people, it would have been denied. Had he asked it of the government, it would have been denied. . . . But it wasn't to these he turned for grace. He turned instead to the bloodied form of the One who hung on the cross next to his and pleaded, "Jesus, remember me when you come into your kingdom." And Jesus answered by saying, "I tell you the truth, today you will be with me in Paradise."

MAX LUCADO

The day of the Lord will come like a thief.

2 PETER 3:10

*P*aul says "we are hoping for something we do not have yet, and we are waiting for it patiently" (Rom. 8:25).

Peter tells us: "You should live holy lives and serve God, as you wait for and look forward to the coming of the day of God" (2 Pet. 3:11–12).

Hope of the future is not a license for irresponsibility in the present. Let us wait forwardly, but let us wait.

In the beginning God created. . . .

GENESIS 1 : 1

A mighty hand went to work. . . .

Out of nothing came light. Out of light came day. . . .

Canyons were carved. Oceans were dug. Mountains erupted out of flatlands. Stars were flung. A universe sparkled.

The hand behind it was mighty.

He is mighty.

MAX LUCADO

*David took [the armor] all off. He took his stick
in his hand and chose five smooth stones from a stream.*

1 SAMUEL 17:39–40

*T*he king tried to give David some equipment.
"What do you want, boy? Shield? Sword? . . ."

David had something else in mind. Five
smooth stones and an ordinary leather sling.

The soldiers gasped. Saul sighed.
Goliath jeered. David swung. And God made
his point. "Anyone who underestimates
what God can do with the ordinary
has rocks in his head."

EVERYDAY BLESSINGS

Where can I flee from your presence? If I go up to the heavens,
you are there; if I make my bed in the depths, you are there.

PSALM 139: 7–8, NIV

Our asking "Where is God?" is like a fish asking "Where is water?" or a bird asking "Where is air?" God is everywhere! Equally present in Peking and Peoria. As active in the lives of Icelanders as in the lives of Texans.

We cannot find a place where God is not.

MAX LUCADO

Do the work of telling the Good News.

2 TIMOTHY 4:5

For every hero in the spotlight, there are dozens in the shadows. They don't get press. They don't draw crowds. They don't even write books! . . .

Behind a rock slide is a pebble. And a revival can begin with one sermon. . . .

Tomorrow's Spurgeon might be mowing your lawn. And the hero who inspires him might be nearer than you think. He might be in your mirror.

Those people who keep their faith until the end will be saved.

M A T T H E W   1 0 : 2 2

*A*re you discouraged as a parent? Hang in there. Are you pessimistic about your job? Roll up your sleeves and go at it again. No communication in your marriage? Give it one more shot. . . .

The Land of Promise, says Jesus, awaits those who endure. It is not just for those who make the victory laps or drink champagne. No sir. The Land of Promise is for those who simply remain to the end.

M A X   L U C A D O

May the Lord lead your hearts
into God's love and Christ's patience.

2 THESSALONIANS 3:5

The majority is not always right. If the majority had ruled, the children of Israel never would have left Egypt. They would have voted to stay in bondage. If the majority had ruled, David never would have fought Goliath. His brothers would have voted for him to stay with the sheep. What's the point? You must listen to your own heart.

God says you're on your way to becoming a disciple when you can keep a clear head and a pure heart.

It takes wisdom to have a good family,
and it takes understanding to make it strong.

PROVERBS 24:3

*D*o you believe in your kids? Then show up. Show up at their games. Show up at their plays. Show up at their recitals. It may not be possible to make each one, but it's sure worth the effort. . . .

Do you believe in your friends? Then show up. Show up at their graduations and weddings. Spend time with them. You want to bring out the best in someone? Then show up.

Godliness with contentment is great gain.

1 TIMOTHY 6:6, NKJV

When we surrender to God the cumbersome sack of discontent, we don't just give up something; we gain something. God replaces it with a lightweight, tailor-made, sorrow-resistant attaché of gratitude.

What will you gain with contentment? You may gain your marriage. You may gain precious hours with your children. You may gain joy.

He delights in mercy. He will again have compassion on us.

MICAH 7:18—19, NKJV

When Joseph was dropped into a pit by his own brothers, God didn't give up.

When Moses said, "Here I am, send Aaron," God didn't give up. . . .

When Peter worshiped Him at the supper and cursed Him at the fire, He didn't give up.

God never gives up.

MAX LUCADO

If you have faith, . . . it will happen.

MATTHEW 21:21

God always rejoices when we dare to dream. In fact, we are much like God when we dream. . . . He wrote the book on making the impossible possible. . . .

Eighty-year-old shepherds don't usually play chicken with Pharoahs . . . but don't tell that to Moses.

Teenage shepherds don't normally have showdowns with giants . . . but don't tell that to David. . . . And for sure don't tell that to God.

EVERYDAY BLESSINGS

When he had finished washing their feet,
he put on his clothes and sat down again.

J O H N   1 3 : 1 2

*P*lease note, he *finished* washing their feet.
That means he left no one out. . . . He washed
the feet of Judas. Jesus washed the feet of his
betrayer. He gave this traitor equal attention.
In just a few hours Judas' feet would guide the
Roman guard to Jesus. But at this moment
they are caressed by Christ. . . .

That's not to say it was easy. . . . That is
to say that God will never call you to do what
he hasn't already done.

Your faith and hope are in God.

1 PETER 1:21, NIV

You will never be completely happy on earth simply because you were not made for earth. Oh, you will have your moments of joy. You will catch glimpses of light. You will know moments or even days of peace. But they simply do not compare with the happiness that lies ahead.

The meek shall inherit the earth,

and shall delight themselves in the abundance of peace.

PSALM 37:11, NKJV

The meek are those who are willing to be used by God. Amazed that God would save them, they are just as surprised that God could use them. They are a junior-high-school clarinet section playing with the Boston Pops. They don't tell the maestro how to conduct; they're just thrilled to be part of the concert.

"I thank God for saving me through Jesus Christ our Lord!"

ROMANS 7:25

Changing the clothes doesn't change the man. Outward discipline doesn't alter what is within. New habits don't make a new soul. That's not to say that outward change is not good. That is to say that outward change is not enough. If one would see the kingdom of God, he must be born again. . . .

The first birth was for earthly life; the second one is for eternal life.

Your life is now hidden with Christ in God.

C O L O S S I A N S   3 : 3 ,   N I V

"*Your life is now hidden with Christ in God.*"
The Chinese language has a great symbol for
this truth. The word for *righteousness* is a
combination of two pictures. On the top is a
lamb. Beneath the lamb is a person. The lamb
covers the person. Isn't that the essence of
righteousness? The Lamb of Christ over the
child of God? Whenever the Father looks
down on you . . . He sees His Son, the perfect
Lamb of God, hiding you.

M A X   L U C A D O

God makes people right with
himself through their faith in Jesus Christ.

ROMANS 3:22

*E*ven if you've fallen, even if you've failed,
even if everyone else has rejected you, Christ
will not turn away from you. He came first
and foremost to those who have no hope.
He goes to those no one else would go to and
says, "I'll give you eternity."

"Follow me," *[Jesus] told him,*
and Matthew got up and followed him.
MATTHEW 9:9, NIV

You gotta wonder what Jesus saw in Matthew. . . .

Whatever it was, it must've been something. Matthew heard the call and never went back. He spent the rest of his life convincing folks that the carpenter was the King. Jesus gave the call and never took it back. He spent his life dying for people like Matthew, convincing a lot of us that if he had a place for Matthew, he just might have a place for us.

MAX LUCADO

We will find grace to help us when we need it.

HEBREWS 4:16, NLT

God isn't going to let you see the distant scene. . . . so you might as well quit looking for it. He promises a lamp unto our feet not a crystal ball into the future. We do not need to know what will happen tomorrow. We only need to know he leads us and "we will find grace to help us when we need it."

"I give my life for the sheep."

JOHN 10:15

*T*he ropes used to tie Our Lord's hands and the soldiers used to lead him to cross were unnecessary. They were incidental. Had they not been there, had there been no trial, no Pilate and no crowd, the very same crucifixion would have occurred. Had Jesus been forced to nail himself to the cross, he would have done it. For it was not the soldiers who killed him, nor the screams of the mob: It was his devotion to us.

MAX LUCADO

If God is for us, who can be against us?

ROMANS 8:32, NKJV

God is for you. Your parents may have forgotten you, your teachers may have neglected you, your siblings may be ashamed of you; but within reach of your prayers is the maker of the oceans. God!

God is for you. Not "may be," not "has been," not "was," not "would be," but "God is!"

There will be one flock and one shepherd.

JOHN 10:16

God has only one flock. Somehow we missed that. Religious division is not his idea. . . . God has one flock. The flock has one shepherd. And though we may think there are many, we are wrong. There is only one.

Never in the Bible are we told to create unity. . . . Paul exhorts us to preserve "the unity which the Spirit gives" (Eph. 4:3, NEB). Our task is not to invent unity, but to acknowledge it.

MAX LUCADO

I can do all things through Christ who strengthens me.

PHILIPPIANS 4 : 13 , NKJV

*R*elax. You have a friend in high places. Does the child of Arnold Schwarzenegger worry about tight pickle-jar lids? Does the son of Nike founder Phil Knight sweat a broken shoestring? . . .

No. Nor should you. The universe's Commander in Chief knows your name. He has walked your streets.

EVERYDAY BLESSINGS

If God so loved us, we also ought to love one another.

1 JOHN 4:11, NKJV

Jesus humbled himself. He went from commanding angels to sleeping in the straw. From holding stars to clutching Mary's finger. The palm that held the universe took the nail of a soldier.

Why? Because that's what love does. It puts the beloved before itself.

MAX LUCADO

JUNE

*God is
abundant in love.*

With God nothing will be impossible.

LUKE 1:37, NKJV

In our world of budgets, long-range planning and computers, don't we find it hard to trust in the unbelievable? Don't most of us tend to scrutinize life behind furrowed brows and walk with cautious steps? It's hard for us to imagine that God can surprise us. To make a little room for miracles today, well, it's not sound thinking. . . .

We forget that "impossible" is one of God's favorite words.

Godliness with contentment is great gain.

1 TIMOTHY 6:6, NKJV

In our world, contentment is a strange street
vendor, roaming . . . slowly from house to
house . . . offering his wares: an hour of peace,
a smile of acceptance, a sigh of relief. . . .

When I asked him why so few welcomed
him into their homes, his answer left me
convicted. "I charge a high price, you know. . . .
I ask people to trade in their schedules,
frustrations, and anxieties. . . . You'd think
I'd have more buyers, . . . but people seem
strangely proud of their ulcers and
headaches."

Watch and pray so that you will not fall into temptation.

MARK 14:38, NIV

"Watch." . . . Keep your eyes open. When you see sin coming, duck. . . . When you sense temptation, go the other way. . . .

"Pray." . . . What prayer does is invite God to walk the shadowy pathways of life with us . . . guarding our backside from the poison darts of the devil.

"Watch and pray." Good advice. Let's take it.

MAX LUCADO

God has . . . all the time in this world and
the next to shower grace and kindness upon us.
EPHESIANS 2:7, THE MESSAGE

God knows everything about you, yet he doesn't hold back his kindness toward you. Has he, knowing all your secrets, retracted one promise or reclaimed one gift?

No, he is kind to you. Why don't you be kind to yourself? He forgives your faults. Why don't you do the same? . . . He believes in you enough to call you his ambassador, his follower, even his child. Why not take his cue and believe in yourself?

I labor, striving according to
His power, which mightily works within me.
COLOSSIANS 1:29, NASB

God was *with* Abraham, even calling the patriarch his friend. . . .

But he is *in* you. With God *in* you, you have a million resources that you did not have before! . . .

Can't stop worrying? Christ can. And he lives within you. Can't forget the past, or forsake your bad habits? Christ can! And he lives within you.

MAX LUCADO

Think only about the things in heaven.

COLOSSIANS 3:2

*E*ngaged people are obsessed with
preparation. The right dress. The right
weight. The right hair and the right tux.
They want everything to be right. Why?
So their fiancée will marry them? No.
Just the opposite. They want to look their best
because their fiancée is marrying them.

The same is true for us. We want to look
our best for Christ. We want our hearts to be
pure and our thoughts to be clean. . . .
We want to be prepared.

"Be happy with me because I found my lost sheep."

LUKE 15:6

When Jesus told the story of the missing sheep, some of the people who were listening wiped away a tear because they knew how it feels to be lost among the crowd. Jesus wanted us to understand that we have a Father who sees and cares for each one of his children—that we are all equally valuable to him.

MAX LUCADO

Surely goodness and mercy shall follow me all the days of my life; and I will dwell in the house of the LORD forever.

PSALM 23:6, NKJV

What a huge statement. Look at the size of it! Goodness and mercy follow the child of God each and every day! Think of the days that lie ahead. What do you see? Days at home with only toddlers? God will be at your side. Days in a dead-end job? He will walk you through. Days of loneliness? He will take your hand. Surely goodness and mercy shall follow me—not some, not most, not nearly all— but *all* the days of my life.

We worked hard all night and caught nothing.

LUKE 5:5, NASB

*D*o you know the feeling of a sleepless, fishless night? Of course you do. For what have you been casting? . . .

Faith? "I want to believe, but . . ."

Healing? "I've been sick so long . . ."

A happy marriage? "No matter what I do . . ."

You've sat where Peter sat. And now Jesus is asking you to go fishing. He knows your nets are empty. He knows your heart is weary. . . .

But he urges, "It's not too late to try again."

MAX LUCADO

The important thing is faith—
the kind of faith that works through love.

GALATIANS 5:6

Symbols are important. Some of them, like communion and baptism, illustrate the cross of Christ. They symbolize salvation . . . but they do not impart salvation.

Putting your trust in a symbol is like claiming to be a sailor because you have a tattoo. . . .

Our God . . . saves us, not because we trust in a symbol, but because we trust in a Savior.

*He will take these dying bodies of ours and change them
into glorious bodies like his own.*

PHILIPPIANS 3:21, TLB

*D*oes this body seem closer to death than
ever before? It should. It is. And unless
Christ comes first, your body will be buried.
Like a seed is placed in the ground, so your
body will be placed in a tomb. And for a
season, your soul will be in heaven while your
body is in the grave. But the seed buried in
the earth will blossom in heaven. Your soul
and body will reunite, and you will be
like Jesus.

As a man rejoices over his
new wife, so your God will rejoice over you.

ISAIAH 62:5

Look long enough into the eyes of our
Savior and, there, . . . you will see a bride.
Dressed in fine linen. Clothed in pure grace.
From the wreath in her hair to the clouds at
her feet, she is royal; she is the princess.
She is the bride. His bride. Walking toward
him, she is not yet with him. But he sees her,
he awaits her, he longs for her.

Mary and Martha sent someone
to tell Jesus, "Lord, the one you love is sick."
JOHN 11:3

*T*he phrase the friend of Lazarus used is worth noting. When he told Jesus of the illness he said, "Lord, the one you love is sick." He doesn't base his appeal on the imperfect love of the one in need, but on the perfect love of the Savior. . . . The power of the prayer, in other words, does not depend on the one who makes the prayer, but on the one who hears the prayer.

MAX LUCADO

Blessed are the meek, for they will inherit the earth.

MATTHEW 5:5, NIV

Matthew 5 is . . . a step-by-step description of how God rebuilds the believer's heart.

The first step is to ask for help— to become "poor in spirit" and admit our need for a Savior.

The next step is sorrow. . . . Those who mourn are those who know they are wrong and say they are sorry. . . .

The next step is the one of renewal: "Blessed are the meek. . . ." Realization of weakness leads to the source of strength—God.

I have made known to you everything I heard from my Father.

JOHN 15:15

We learn brevity from Jesus. His greatest sermon can be read in eight minutes (Matt. 5–7). . . . He summarized prayer in five phrases (Matt. 6:9–13). He silenced accusers with one challenge (John 8:7). He rescued a soul with one sentence (Luke 23:43). He summarized the Law in three verses (Mark 12:29–31), and he reduced all his teachings to one command (John 15:12).

He made his point and went home.

MAX LUCADO

*We are made holy through the
sacrifice Christ made in his body once and for all time.*

HEBREWS 10:10

The Son of God became the Lamb of God,
the cross became the altar, and we were made
holy through the sacrifice Christ made in His
body once and for all time.

What needed to be paid was paid. What
had to be done was done. Innocent blood was
required. Innocent blood was offered, once
and for all time. Bury those five words deep
in your heart. *Once and for all time.*

God gives us a free gift—life forever in Christ Jesus our Lord.

ROMANS 6:23

One of the hardest things to do is to be saved by grace. There's something in us that reacts to God's free gift. We have some weird compulsion to create laws, systems, and regulations that will make us "worthy" of our gift.

Why do we do that? The only reason I can figure is pride. To accept grace means to accept its necessity, and most folks don't like to do that. To accept grace also means that one realizes his despair, and most people aren't too keen on doing that either.

MAX LUCADO

Love covers a multitude of sins.

1 PETER 4:8, NASB

*H*ave you ever heard anyone gossip about someone you know? . . . What do you have to say?

Here is what love says: Love says nothing. Love stays silent. "Love covers a multitude of sins." Love doesn't expose. It doesn't gossip. If love says anything, love speaks words of defense. Words of kindness. Words of protection.

*Those who believe in God will be
careful to use their lives for doing good.*

TITUS 3:8

*B*eing busy is not a sin. Jesus was busy.
Paul was busy. Peter was busy. Nothing of
significance is achieved without effort and
hard work and weariness. That, in and of
itself, is not a sin. But being busy in an
endless pursuit of *things* that leave us empty
and hollow and broken inside—that cannot be
pleasing to God.

MAX LUCADO

After I go and prepare a place for you,
I will come back and take you to be with me.

JOHN 14:3

Note the promise of Jesus. "I will come back and take you to be with me." Jesus pledges to take us home. He does not delegate this task. He may send missionaries to teach you, angels to protect you, teachers to guide you, singers to inspire you, and physicians to heal you, but He sends no one to take you. He reserves this job for Himself.

He will destroy death forever.

ISAIAH 25:8

*J*esus explained that the river of death was nothing to fear. The people wouldn't believe him. He touched a boy and called him back to life. . . . He let a dead man spend four days in a grave and then called him out. Is that enough? Apparently not. For it was necessary for him to . . . submerge himself in the water of death before people would believe that death had been conquered.

After he . . . came out on the other side of death's river, . . . it was time to celebrate.

MAX LUCADO

"If you believe, you will get anything you ask for in prayer."

MATTHEW 21:22

Don't reduce this grand statement to the category of new cars and paychecks. . . .

God wants you to fly. He wants you to fly free of yesterday's guilt. He wants you to fly free of today's fears. He wants you to fly free of tomorrow's grave. Sin, fear, and death. These are the mountains he has moved. These are the prayers he will answer.

Thank you for your love, thank you for your faithfulness.
PSALM 138:2, THE MESSAGE

We give more applause to a brawny ball-carrier than we do to the God who made us. We sing more songs to the moon than to the Christ who saved us. . . .

Though we may not act like our Father, there is no greater truth than this: We are his. Unalterably. He loves us. Undyingly.

God has planted eternity in the hearts of men.

ECCLESIASTES 3:10, TLB

You will never be completely happy on earth
simply because you were not made for earth.
Oh, you will have you moments of joy.
You will catch glimpses of light. You will
know moments or even days of peace.
But they simply do not compare with the
happiness that lies ahead.

Everyone must die once and be judged.

HEBREWS 9:27

*E*ternity is to be taken seriously. A judgment is coming.

Our task on earth is singular—to choose our eternal home. You can afford many wrong choices in life. You can choose the wrong career and survive, the wrong city and survive, the wrong house and survive. You can even choose the wrong mate and survive. But there is one choice that must be made correctly and that is your eternal destiny.

MAX LUCADO

If anyone belongs to Christ, there is a new creation.

2 CORINTHIANS 5:17

At our new birth God remakes our souls and gives us what we need, again. New eyes so we can see by faith. A new mind so we can have the mind of Christ. New strength so we won't grow tired. A new vision so we won't lose heart. A new voice for praise and new hands for service. And most of all, a new heart. A heart that has been cleansed by Christ.

All of you who were baptized
into Christ have clothed yourselves with Christ.

GALATIANS 3:27, NIV

We wear Jesus. And those who don't believe in Jesus note that we do. They make decisions about Christ by watching us. When we are kind, they assume Christ is kind. When we are gracious, they assume Christ is gracious. But if we are brash, what will people think about our King? When we are dishonest, what assumptions will an observer make about our Master? . . . Courteous conduct honors Christ.

MAX LUCADO

I will pour out my Spirit on all kinds of people.

ACTS 2:17

On the surface they appear no different. Peter is still brazen. Nathanael is still reflective. Philip is still calculating.

They look the same. But they aren't. . . .

Within them dwells a fire not found on earth. Christ has taught them. The Father has forgiven them. The Spirit indwells them. They are not the same. And because they are different, so is the world.

Man shall not live on bread alone,
but on every word that proceeds out of the mouth of God.

MATTHEW 4:4, NASB

*T*rust God's Word. Don't trust your
emotions. Don't trust your opinions.
Don't even trust your friends. . . .

Jesus told Satan, "Man shall not live on
bread alone, but on every word that proceeds
out of the mouth of God." The verb *proceeds* is
literally "pouring out." Its tense suggests
that God is constantly and aggressively
communicating with the world through his
Word. God is speaking still!

MAX LUCADO

The good man brings good things
out of the good stored up in his heart.

LUKE 6:45, NIV

When you are offered a morsel of gossip marinated in slander, do you turn it down or pass it on? That depends on the state of your heart. . . .

The state of your heart dictates whether you harbor a grudge or give grace, seek self-pity or seek Christ, drink human misery or taste God's mercy.

*Love is
only love if chosen.*

Let us love one another, for love is of God.

1 JOHN 4:7, NKJV

Long to be more loving? Begin by accepting your place as a dearly loved child. "Be imitators of God, therefore, as dearly loved children" (Eph. 5:1, NIV).

Want to learn to forgive? Then consider how you've been forgiven. "Be kind and compassionate to one another, forgiving each other, just as in Christ God forgave you" (Eph. 4:32, NIV).

He willingly gave his life. . . .
He carried away the sins of many people.

ISAIAH 53:12

You can't go to the cross with just your head
and not your heart. It doesn't work that way.
Calvary is not a mental trip. It's not an
intellectual exercise. . . .

It's a heart-splitting hour of emotion. . . .

That's *God* on that cross. It's us who put
him there.

While we were still sinners, Christ died for us.

ROMANS 5:8, NIV

When we love with expectations, we say, "I love you. But I'll love you even more if . . ."

Christ's love had none of this. No strings, no expectations, no hidden agendas, no secrets. His love for us was, and is, up front and clear. "I love you," he says. "Even if you let me down. I love you in spite of your failures."

MAX LUCADO

*Do not merely look out for your own
personal interests, but also for the interests of others.*

PHILIPPIANS 2:4, NASB

What's the cure for selfishness?

Get your self out of your eye by getting your eye off your self. Quit staring at that little self, and focus on your great Savior. . . .

Focus on the encouragement in Christ, the consolation of Christ, the love of Christ, the fellowship of the Spirit, the affection and compassion of heaven.

Jesus had to be made like his brothers . . .
so he could be their merciful and faithful high priest.

HEBREWS 2:17

Jesus displays the bad apples of his family tree in the first chapter of the New Testament. . . . Rahab was a Jericho harlot. . . . David had a personality as irregular as a Picasso painting—one day writing psalms, another day seducing his captain's wife. But did Jesus erase his name from the list? Not at all. . . .

If your family tree has bruised fruit, then Jesus wants you to know, "I've been there."

This is the victory that conquers the world—our faith.

1 JOHN 5:4

What is unique about the kingdom of God is that you are assured of victory. You have won!

If you have no faith in the future, then you have no power in the present. If you have no faith in the life beyond this life, then your present life is going to be powerless. But if you believe in the future and are assured of victory, then there should be a dance in your step and a smile on your face.

I will dwell in the house of the LORD forever.

PSALM 23:6, NKJV

Where will you live forever? In the house of the Lord. If his house is your "forever house," what does that make this earthly house? You got it! Short-term housing. This is not our home.

This explains the homesickness we feel. . . . Deep down you know you are not home yet. So be careful not to act like you are.

MAX LUCADO

It is not our love for God; it is God's love for us
in sending his Son to be the way to take away our sins.

1 JOHN 4:10

*P*lease note: Salvation is God-given,
God-driven, God empowered, and God-
originated. The gift is not from man to God.
It is from God to man. . . .

Grace is created by God and given to man.

*Be faithful, even if you have
to die, and I will give you the crown of life.*

REVELATION 2:10

Can you imagine a world with no death,
only life? If you can, you can imagine heaven.
For citizens of heaven wear the crown of life. . . .

We are not made of steel, we are made of
dust. And this life is not crowned with life,
it is crowned with death.

The next life, however, is different.

MAX LUCADO

You were taught to be made new
in your hearts, to become a new person.

E P H E S I A N S 4 : 2 3

What if, for one day and one night, Jesus lives your life with his heart? Your heart gets the day off, and your life is led by the heart of Christ. His priorities govern your actions. His passions drive your decisions. His love directs your behavior. . . .

Would people notice a change? . . . Would you still do what you had planned to do for the next twenty-four hours?

It is impossible for the blood of bulls and goats to take away sins.

HEBREWS 10:4, NIV

Sacrifices could offer temporary solutions,
but only God could offer the eternal one.

So he did.

Beneath the rubble of a fallen world,
he pierced his hands. In the wreckage of a
collapsed humanity, he ripped open his
side. . . . He gave his blood.

It was all he had.

MAX LUCADO

We must not become tired of doing good.

GALATIANS 6:9

When we are mistreated, our animalistic response is to go on the hunt. Instinctively, we double up our fists. Getting even is only natural. Which, incidentally, is precisely the problem. Revenge is natural, not spiritual. Getting even is the rule of the jungle. Giving grace is the rule of the kingdom. . . .

To forgive someone is to admit our limitations. We've been given only one piece of life's jigsaw puzzle. Only God has the cover of the box.

All of you who were baptized into
Christ have clothed yourselves with Christ.

G A L A T I A N S   3 : 2 7 ,   N I V

While on the cross, Jesus felt the indignity and disgrace of a criminal. No, He was not guilty. No, He had not committed a sin. And, no, He did not deserve to be sentenced. But you and I were, we had, and we did.

Though we come to the cross dressed in sin, we leave the cross dressed in "garments of salvation" (Isa. 61:10, NIV). Indeed, we leave dressed in Christ Himself.

*We do not live following our
sinful selves, but we live following the Spirit.*

ROMANS 8:4

ALMOST. How many times do these six ugly letters find their way into despairing epitaphs?

"She almost chose not to leave him." . . . "He almost became a Christian." . . .

Jesus . . . demands absolute obedience. He never has had room for "almost" in his vocabulary. You are either with him or against him. . . . With the Master, "almost" is just as good as "never."

The LORD has done great things for us, and we are glad.

PSALM 126:3, NKJV

You have not been sprinkled with forgiveness. You have not been spattered with grace. You have not been dusted with kindness. You have been immersed in it. You are submerged in mercy. You are a minnow in the ocean of God's mercy. Let it change you!

MAX LUCADO

Unfriendly people are selfish.

PROVERBS 18:1

We're in a fast-moving, fast-paced society. We need to build bridges between our hearts and those of people we see who need a friend—and allow Jesus to cross that bridge of friendship and walk into their lives. . . .

Whether or not you are friendly could determine whether or not someone hears about Jesus.

The LORD our God is right in everything he does.

DANIEL 9:14

God is never wrong. He has never rendered a wrong decision, experienced the wrong attitude, taken the wrong path, said the wrong thing, or acted the wrong way. He is never too late or too early, too loud or too soft, too fast or too slow. He has always been and always will be right. He is righteous.

MAX LUCADO

Remember Jesus Christ,
raised from the dead, descended from David.

2 TIMOTHY 2:8, NIV

In a letter written within earshot of the sharpening of the blade that would sever his head, Paul urged Timothy to "Remember Jesus Christ, raised from the dead, descended from David. . . ."

Remember the dead called from the grave with a Galilean accent. Remember the eyes of God that wept human tears. And, most of all, remember this descendant of David who beat the hell out of death.

Jesus said, "Come."

MATTHEW 14:29

You can't read anything about God without finding him issuing invitations. He invited Eve to marry Adam, the animals to enter the ark, David to be king, Israel to leave bondage, Nehemiah to rebuild Jerusalem. God is an inviting God. He invited Mary to birth his son, the disciples to fish for men, the adulterous woman to start over, and Thomas to touch his wounds. God is the King who prepares the palace, sets the table, and invites his subjects to come in.

MAX LUCADO

Your life is a journey you must
travel with a deep consciousness of God.

1 PETER 1:17, THE MESSAGE

*E*ach life is . . . a story to be written.
The Author starts each life story, but each life
will write his or her own ending.

What a dangerous liberty. How much
safer it would have been to finish the story for
each Adam. To script every opinion. It would
have been simpler. It would have been safer.
But it would not have been love.
Love is only love
if chosen.

Serve only the LORD your God.
Respect him, keep his commands, and obey him.

DEUTERONOMY 13:4

Christ's kingdom is . . . a kingdom where membership is *granted*, not *purchased.* You are placed into God's kingdom. *You* are "adopted." And this occurs not when you do enough, but when you admit you can't do enough. You don't earn it; you simply accept it. As a result, you serve, not out of arrogance or fear, but out of gratitude.

MAX LUCADO

We have an Advocate with the Father, Jesus Christ the righteous.

1 JOHN 2:1, NASB

*E*ven in heaven, Christ remains our next door Savior. . . . The King of the universe commands comets with a human tongue and directs celestial traffic with a human hand. Still human. Still divine. Living forever through his two natures. . . .

The hands that blessed the bread of the boy now bless the prayers of the millions. . . . You know what this means? The greatest force in the cosmos understands and intercedes for you.

*"Anything you did for even the
least of my people here, you also did for me."*

MATTHEW 25:40

What is the sign of the saved? Their scholarship? Their willingness to go to foreign lands? Their ability to amass an audience and preach? Their skillful pens and hope-filled volumes? . . . No.

The sign of the saved is their love for the least. . . .

No fanfare. No hoopla. No media coverage. Just good people doing good things. For when we do good things to others we do good things to God.

God is being patient with you. . . .
He wants all people to change their hearts and lives.

2 PETER 3:9

In many ways your new birth is like your first:
In your new birth God provides what you
need; someone else feels the pain, and
someone else does the work. And just as
parents are patient with their newborn,
so God is patient with you. But there is one
difference. The first time you had no choice
about being born; this time you do. The power
is God's. The effort is God's. The pain is
God's. But the choice is yours.

The LORD God is like a sun and shield;
the LORD gives us kindness and honor.

PSALM 84:11

Rejections are like speed bumps on the road. They come with the journey. . . . You can't keep people from rejecting you. But you can keep rejections from enraging you. How? By letting God's acceptance compensate for their rejection.

When others reject you, let God accept you. He is not frowning. He is not mad. He sings over you. Take a long drink from His limitless love.

MAX LUCADO

We have freedom now, because Christ made us free.

GALATIANS 5:1

*S*ome teach that we earn God's favor by what we know (intellectualism). Others insist we are saved by what we do (moralism). Still others claim that salvation is determined by what we feel (emotionalism).

However you package it, Paul contests, . . . salvation comes only through the cross— no additions, no alterations.

Take courage, it is I; do not be afraid.

MATTHEW 14:27, NASB

Waves slapping his waist and rain stinging his face. Jesus speaks to [the disciples] at once. "Courage! I am! Don't be afraid!"

Speaking from a burning bush to a knee-knocking Moses, God announced, "I AM WHO I AM" (Exod. 3:14, NASB).

God gets into things! Red Seas. . . . Judean wildernesses, weddings, funerals, and Galilean tempests. Look and you'll find what everyone from Moses to Martha discovered. God in the middle of our storms.

MAX LUCADO

*Faith is being sure of what we hope
for and certain of what we do not see.*

*F*aith is trusting what the eye can't see.

Eyes see the prowling lion. Faith sees Daniel's angel.

Eyes see storms. Faith sees Noah's rainbow.

Your eyes see your faults. Your faith sees your Savior.

Your eyes see your guilt. Your faith sees his blood.

Anyone who has seen me has seen the Father.

JOHN 14:9, NIV

Only in seeing his Maker does a man truly become man. For in seeing his Creator man catches a glimpse of what he was intended to be. He who would see his God would then see the reason for death and the purpose of time. Destiny? Tomorrow? Truth? All are questions within the reach of the man who knows his source.

It is in seeing Jesus that man sees his Source.

MAX LUCADO

Come, see where his body was lying.

MATTHEW 28:6, NLT

Take a look at the vacated tomb. Did you know the opponents of Christ never challenged its vacancy? No Pharisee or Roman soldier ever led a contingent back to the burial site and declared, "The angel was wrong. The body is here. It was all a rumor." . . .

Helps explain the Jerusalem revival. When the apostles argued for the empty tomb, the people looked to the Pharisees for a rebuttal. But they had none to give.

Our homeland is in heaven, and we are waiting
for our Savior, the Lord Jesus Christ, to come from heaven.

PHILIPPIANS 3:20

You've seen people treat this world like it was a permanent home. It's not. You've seen people pour time and energy into life like it will last forever. It won't. You've seen people so proud of what they have done, that they hope they will never have to leave—they will.

We all will. We are in transit.

MAX LUCADO

AUGUST

God is nearer
than you think.

I want to know Christ.

PHILIPPIANS 3:10

*T*he Fort Knox of faith is Christ. Fellowship with him. Walking with him. Pondering him. Exploring him. The heart-stopping realization that in him you are part of something ancient, endless, unstoppable, and unfathomable. And that he, who can dig the Grand Canyon with his pinkie, thinks you're worth his death on Roman timber. Christ is the reward of Christianity.

MAX LUCADO

GOD is great, and worth a thousand Hallelujahs.

PSALM 96:4, THE MESSAGE

Never did the obscene come so close to the holy as it did on Calvary. Never did the good in the world so intertwine with the bad as it did on the cross. Never did what is right involve itself so intimately with what is wrong, as it did when Jesus was suspended between heaven and earth.

God on a cross. Humanity at its worst. Divinity at its best.

Love is patient.

1 CORINTHIANS 13:4

The Greek word used here for patient . . . means "taking a long time to boil."

Think about a pot of boiling water. . . . Water boils quickly when the flame is high. It boils slowly when the flame is low. Patience "keeps the burner down." . . .

Patience isn't naive. It doesn't ignore misbehavior. It just keeps the flame low. It waits. It listens. . . . This is how God treats us. And, according to Jesus, this is how we should treat others.

MAX LUCADO

He is able . . . to run to the cry of
. . . those who are being . . . tested.

HEBREWS 2:18, AMP

*J*esus was angry enough to purge the temple,
hungry enough to eat raw grain, distraught
enough to weep in public, fun loving enough
to be called a drunkard, winsome enough to
attract kids, . . . radical enough to get kicked
out of town, responsible enough to care for his
mother, tempted enough to know the smell of
Satan, and fearful enough to sweat blood. . . .

Whatever you are facing, he knows how
you feel.

LORD, you bless those who do what is right.

PSALM 5:12

The trip from Egypt to the promised land can be made in nine days (Deut. 1:2). It took the Israelites thirty-eight years.

What they should have done, they didn't. . . . So God decided they needed some time to rethink a few things.

Maybe God is wanting to teach you a few things. Pay attention. You don't want to spend thirty-eight years missing the point.

God, we thank you; we thank you because you are near.

PSALM 75:1

God is the God who follows. I wonder . . . have you sensed him following you? We often miss him. . . . We don't know our Helper when he is near. But he comes.

Through the kindness of a stranger. The majesty of a sunset. . . . Through a word well spoken or a touch well timed, have you sensed his presence?

Jesus is coming with the clouds, and everyone will see him.
REVELATION 1:7

Every person who has ever lived will be present at that final gathering. Every heart that has ever beat. Every mouth that has ever spoken. On that day you will be surrounded by a sea of people. Rich, poor. Famous, unknown. Kings, bums. Brilliant, demented. All will be present. And all will be looking in one direction. All will be looking at Him—the Son of Man. Wrapped in splendor. Shot through with radiance.

A person is made right with God through faith.

ROMANS 3:28

*D*are you stand before God and ask him to save you because of your suffering or your sacrifice or your tears or your study? . . .

Nor did Paul. It took him decades to discover what he wrote in only one sentence.

"A person is made right with God through faith" Not through good works, suffering, or study. All those may be the result of salvation but they are not the cause of it.

The blood of Jesus, God's Son, cleanses us from every sin.

1 JOHN 1:7

The cleansing is not a promise for the future but a reality in the present. Let a speck of dust fall on the soul of a saint, and it is washed away. Let a spot of filth land on the heart of God's child, and the filth is wiped away. . . .

Our Savior kneels down and gazes upon the darkest acts of our lives. But rather than recoil in horror, he reaches out in kindness and says, "I can clean that if you want."

MAX LUCADO

*Blessed are those who hunger and
thirst for righteousness, for they will be filled.*

MATTHEW 5:6, NIV

We usually get what we hunger and thirst
for. The problem is, the treasures of earth
don't satisfy. The promise is, the treasures of
heaven do. . . .

Blessed are those who, if everything they
own were taken from them, would be, at
most, inconvenienced, because their true
wealth is elsewhere.

*The teaching I ask you to accept
is easy; the load I give you to carry is light.*

MATTHEW 11:30

Jesus says he is the solution for weariness
of soul.

Go to him. Be honest with him. Admit
you have soul secrets you've never dealt with.
He already knows what they are. He's just
waiting for you to ask him to help. . . .

Go ahead. You'll be glad you did.
Those near to you will be glad as well.

MAX LUCADO

There is one God and one mediator
between God and men, the man Christ Jesus.

1 TIMOTHY 2:5, NIV

Somewhere, sometime, somehow you got tangled up in garbage, and you've been avoiding God. You've allowed a veil of guilt to come between you and your Father. You wonder if you could ever feel close to God again.

God welcomes you. God is not avoiding you. God is not resisting you. The door is open, and God invites you in.

The Word was with God, and the Word was God.

JOHN 1:1

I've always perceived [the apostle] John as a fellow who viewed life simply. . . .

For example, defining Jesus would be a challenge to the best of writers, but John handles the task with casual analogy. The Messiah, in a word, was "the Word." A walking message. A love letter. Be he a fiery verb or a tender adjective, he was, quite simply, a word.

MAX LUCADO

Pile your troubles on GOD's shoulders—he'll carry your load.

PSALM 55:22, THE MESSAGE

I wonder, how many burdens is Jesus carrying for us that we know nothing about? We're aware of some. He carries our sin. He carries our shame. He carries our eternal debt. But are there others? Has He lifted fears before we felt them? . . . Those times when we have been surprised by our own sense of peace? Could it be that Jesus has lifted our anxiety onto His shoulders and placed a yoke of kindness on ours?

Walk out into the daylight sober, dressed up in faith, love, and the hope of salvation.

1 THESSALONIANS 5:8, THE MESSAGE

Don't put your hope into things that change—relationships, money, talents, beauty, even health. Set your sights on the one thing that can never change: trust in your heavenly Father.

MAX LUCADO

The cross of our Lord Jesus Christ is my only reason for bragging.

GALATIANS 6:14

*D*o you feel a need for affirmation?
Does your self-esteem need attention?
You don't need to drop names or show off.
You need only pause at the base of the cross
and be reminded of this: The maker of the
stars would rather die for you than live
without you. And that is a fact. So if you need
to brag, brag about that.

You knit me together in my mother's womb.

PSALM 139:13, NIV

"Knitted together" is how the psalmist described the process of God making man. Not manufactured or mass-produced, but knitted. Each thread of personality tenderly intertwined. Each string of temperament deliberately selected. . . .

The Creator, the master weaver, threading together the soul.

Each one different. No two alike. None identical.

"What do you think about the Christ?

MATTHEW 22:42

The idea that a virgin would be selected by God to bear himself. . . . The notion that God would don a scalp and toes and two eyes. . . . The thought that the King of the universe would sneeze and burp and get bit by mosquitoes. . . . It's too incredible. Too revolutionary. We would never create such a Savior. We aren't that daring.

"He put mud on my eyes, I washed, and now I see."

JOHN 9:15

It isn't the circumstance that matters; it is God in the circumstance. It isn't the words; it is God speaking them. it wasn't the mud that healed the eyes of the blind man; it was the finger of God in the mud. The cradle and the cross were as common as grass. What made them holy was the One laid upon them.

I lay down my life. . . . No one takes it from Me.

JOHN 10:17–18, NKJV

*J*esus knows the meaning of the phrase, "It's just not right."

For it wasn't right that people spit into the eyes that had wept for them. It wasn't right that soldiers ripped chunks of flesh out of he back of their God. It wasn't right that spikes pierced the hands that formed the earth. . . .

Was it right? No. . . . Was it love? Yes.

The One who comes from above is greater than all.

JOHN 3:31

"They have no more wine," Mary told Jesus
(John 2:3). That's it. That's all she said.
She didn't go ballistic. She simply assessed the
problem and gave it to Christ. . . .

Next time you face a common calamity,
follow Mary's example: Identify the problem.
(You'll half-solve it.) Present it to Jesus.
(He's happy to help.) Do what he says.
(No matter how crazy.)

*LORD, teach me what you want
me to do, and I will live by your truth.*

PSALM 86:11

When kindness comes grudgingly,
we'll remember God's kindness to us and ask
Him to make us more kind. When patience is
scarce, we'll thank Him for His and ask Him
to make us more patient. When it's hard to
forgive, we won't list all the times we've been
given grief. Rather, we'll list all the times
we've been given grace and pray to
become more forgiving.

[Jesus] died so he could give the church to himself
like a bride in all her beauty . . . pure and without fault.

EPHESIANS 5:27

From our perspective, the church isn't so
pretty. We see the backbiting, the squabbling,
the divisions. Heaven sees that, as well.
But heaven sees more. Heaven sees the church
as cleansed and made holy by Christ.

Heaven sees the church ascending to
heaven. Heaven sees the Bride wearing the
spotless gown of Jesus Christ.

MAX LUCADO

Jesus Christ is the same yesterday, today, and forever.

HEBREWS 13:8, NLT

The present-tense Christ. He never says, "I was." We do. We do because "we were." We were younger, faster, prettier. Prone to be people of the past tense, we reminisce. Not God. Unwavering in strength, he need never say, "I was." Heaven has no rearview mirrors. . . .

Can God be more God? No. He does not change. He is the "I am" God. "Jesus Christ is the same yesterday, today, and forever."

You thrill to GOD's Word, you chew on Scripture day and night.
PSALM 1:1–2, THE MESSAGE

The Bible is not a newspaper to be skimmed but rather a mine to be quarried.

Here is a practical point. Study the Bible a little at a time. God seems to send messages as he did his manna: one day's portion at a time. He provides "a command here, a command there. A rule here, a rule there. A little lesson here, a little lesson there" (Isa. 28:10). Choose depth over quantity.

MAX LUCADO

He forgives your sins—every one.

PSALM 103:3, THE MESSAGE

*I*t's against God's nature to remember forgiven sins. . . .

He who is perfect love cannot hold grudges. If he does, then he isn't perfect love. And if he isn't perfect love, you might as well put this book down and go fishing, because both of us are chasing fairy tales.

But I believe in his loving forgetfulness. And I believe he has a graciously terrible memory.

*"I gave you this work: to go
and produce fruit, fruit that will last."*

JOHN 15:16

A good gardener will do what it takes to
help a vine bear fruit. What fruit does God
want? Love, joy, peace, patience, kindness,
goodness, faithfulness, gentleness, and self-
control (Gal. 5:22–23). These are the fruits
of the Spirit. And this is what God longs to
see in us. And like a careful gardener, he will
clip and cut away anything that interferes.

MAX LUCADO

Let us fix our eyes on Jesus, the author and perfecter
of our faith, who for the joy set before him endured the cross.

*R*emember, heaven was not foreign to Jesus. He is the only person to live on earth *after* he had lived in heaven. . . . He knew heaven before he came to earth. He knew what awaited him upon his return. And knowing what awaited him in heaven enabled him to bear the shame on earth.

Whoever is wise will . . . think about the love of the LORD.

PSALM 107:43

Aging? A necessary process to pass on to a better world.

Death? Merely a brief passage, a tunnel. . . .

The next time you find yourself alone in a dark alley facing the undeniables of life, don't cover them with a blanket, or ignore them with a nervous grin. Don't turn up the TV and pretend they aren't there. Instead, stand still, whisper God's name, and listen. He is nearer than you think.

MAX LUCADO

"I am the voice of one calling out in the desert."

JOHN 1:23

John was a voice for Christ with more than his voice. His life matched his words. When a person's ways and words are the same, the fusion is explosive. But when a person says one thing and lives another, the result is destructive. People will know we are Christians, not because we bear the name, but because we live the life.

When the Lord Jesus comes . . . all the
people who have believed will be amazed at Jesus.

2 THESSALONIANS 1:10

*A*mazed at Jesus. . . . Paul doesn't measure the
joy of encountering the apostles or embracing
our loved ones. If we will be amazed at these,
which certainly we will, he does not say. What
he does say is that we will be amazed at Jesus.

What we have only seen in our thoughts,
we will see with our eyes. . . . What we've seen
in a glimpse, we will then see in full view.
And . . . we will be amazed.

MAX LUCADO

*God loves those
who need him most.*

You answer us in amazing ways, God our Savior.

PSALM 65:5

God never turns his back on those who ask honest questions. He never did in the Old Testament; he never did in the New Testament. So if you are asking honest questions of God, he will not turn away from you. . . .

In learning to depend on God, we must accept that we may not know all the answers, but we know *who* knows the answers.

MAX LUCADO

From everlasting to everlasting you are God.

PSALM 90:2, NIV

You and I need a middle C. Haven't you had enough change in your life? Relationships change. Health changes. The weather changes. But the Yahweh who ruled the earth last night is the same Yahweh who rules it today. Same convictions. Same plan. Same mood. Same love. He never changes. You can no more alter God than a pebble can alter the rhythm of the Pacific. Yahweh is our Middle C. A still point in a turning world.

A person is made right with God not by following the law,
but by trusting in Jesus Christ.

GALATIANS 2:16

God is not stumped by an evil world. He doesn't gasp in amazement at the depth of our faith or the depth of our failures. We can't surprise God with our cruelties. He knows the condition of the world . . . and loves it just the same. For just when we find a place where God would never be (like on a cross), we look again and there he is, in the flesh.

MAX LUCADO

GOD's strong name is our help.

PSALM 124:8, THE MESSAGE

You have a ticket to heaven no thief can take,
an eternal home no divorce can break.
Every sin of your life has been cast to the sea.
Every mistake you've made is nailed to the tree.
You're blood-bought and heaven-made.
A child of God—forever saved.
So be grateful, joyful—for isn't it true?
What you don't have is much less
than what you do.

When they had done this, they caught so many
fish that their nets were beginning to break.

LUKE 5:6, NRSV

*P*eter's arm is yanked into the water. It's all
he can do to hang on until the other guys can
help. Within moments the four fishermen
and the carpenter are up to their knees in
flopping silver.

Peter lifts his eyes off the catch and onto
the face of Christ. In that moment, for the
first time, he sees Jesus. Not Jesus the Fish
Finder. . . . Not Jesus the Rabbi. Peter sees
Jesus the Lord.

*There is therefore now no condemnation to those
who are in Christ Jesus, . . . who walk according to the Spirit.*

ROMANS 8:1, NKJV

*D*oes the Word of God say, "There is *limited*
condemnation for those who are in Christ
Jesus"? No. Does it say, "There is *some*
condemnation . . ."? No. It says, "There is *no*
condemnation for those who are in Christ
Jesus." Think of it—regardless of our sin,
we are not guilty!

My cup overflows with blessings.

PSALM 23:5, NLT

Is an overflowing cup full? Absolutely. The wine reaches the rim and then tumbles over the edge. The goblet is not large enough to contain the quantity. According to David, our hearts are not large enough to contain the blessings that God wants to give. He pours and pours until they literally flow over the edge and down on the table. . . .

The last thing we need to worry about is not having enough. Our cup overflows with blessings.

MAX LUCADO

You have been born again, not of perishable seed, but of imperishable, through the living and enduring word of God.

1 PETER 1:23, NIV

We are free either to love God or not. He invites us to love Him. He urges us to love Him. He came that we might love Him. But, in the end, the choice is yours and mine. To take that choice from each of us, for Him to force us to love Him, would be less than love. . . .

He leaves the choice to us.

How can we who died to sin still live in it?

R O M A N S   6 : 2 ,   R S V

*H*ow can we who have been made right not live righteous lives? How can we who have been loved not love? How can we who have been blessed not bless? How can we who have been given grace not live graciously? . . .

How could grace result in anything but gracious living? "So do you think we should continue sinning so that God will give us even more grace? No!" (Rom. 6:1, NCV).

M A X   L U C A D O

His head and hair were white like wool,
as white as snow, and his eyes were like flames of fire.

REVELATION 1:14

What would a person look like if he had never sinned? If no worry wrinkled his brow and no anger shadowed his eyes? If no bitterness snarled his lips and no selfishness bowed his smile? Is a person had never sinned, how would he appear? We'll know when we see Jesus.

Do good to me, your servant,
so I can live, so I can obey your word.

PSALM 119:17

God loves to decorate. God *has* to decorate. Let Him live long enough in a heart, and that heart will begin to change. Portraits of hurt will be replaced by landscapes of grace. Walls of anger will be demolished and shaky foundations restored. God can no more leave a life unchanged than a mother can leave her child's tear untouched.

MAX LUCADO

This is my command: Love each other.

JOHN 15:17

*R*esentment is when you let your hurt
become hate. Resentment is when you allow
what is eating you to eat you up. Resentment
is when you poke, stoke, feed, and fan the fire,
stirring the flames and reliving the pain. . . .

Revenge is the raging fire. . . . Bitterness
is the trap that snares. . . . And mercy is the
choice that can set them all free.

Create in me a new heart, O God.

PSALM 51:10, TLB

*E*ver blamed your plight on Washington? (If they'd lower the tax rates, my business would work.) Inculpated your family for your failure? (Mom always liked my sister more.) . . .

Consider the prayer of David: "Create *in* me a new heart, O God." . . .

Real change is an inside job. You might alter things a day or two with money and systems, but the heart of the matter is and always will be, the matter of the heart.

MAX LUCADO

Surely he took up our infirmities and carried our sorrows.

ISAIAH 53:4, NIV

Why did Jesus live on earth as long as he did? Why not step into our world just long enough to die for our sins and then leave? Why not a sinless year or week? Why did He have to live a life? To take on our sins is one thing, but to take on our sunburns, our sore throats? To experience death, yes—but to put up with life? To put up with long roads, long days, and short tempers? Why did he do it?

Because He wants you to trust Him.

The Word became flesh and made his dwelling among us.

JOHN 1:14, NIV

The one to whom we pray knows our feelings. He knows temptation. He has felt discouraged. He has been hungry and sleepy and tired. . . . He nods in understanding when we pray in anger. . . . He smiles when we confess our weariness. . . .

He, too, knew the drone of the humdrum and the weariness that comes with long days. . . . God became flesh and dwelt among us.

*God loved us, and through his grace he gave us
a good hope and encouragement that continues forever.*

2 THESSALONIANS 2:17

God loves those who need him most, who rely on him, depend on him, and trust him in everything. Little he cares whether you've been as pure as John or as sinful as Mary Magdalene. All that matters is your trust in him.

"I will feed My flock, and I will make them lie down," says the Lord GOD.

EZEKIEL 34:15, NKJV

What the shepherd does with the flock, our Shepherd will do with us. He will lead us to the high country. When the pasture is bare down here. God will lead us up there. He will guide us through the gate, out of the flatlands, and up the path of the mountain.

MAX LUCADO

*"I have questioned him before
you all, and I have not found him guilty."*

LUKE 23:14

A crook places himself between Jesus and
the accusers and speaks on his behalf. . . .
"We are getting what our deeds deserve.
But this man has done nothing wrong"
(Luke 23:41, NIV).

We are guilty and he is innocent.

We are filthy and he is pure.

We are wrong and he is right.

He is not on that cross for his sins. He is
there for ours.

The LORD will arise over you,
and His glory will be seen upon you.

ISAIAH 60:2, NKJV

When we create a redeemer, we keep him safely distant in his faraway castle. We allow him only the briefest of encounters with us. We permit him to swoop in and out with his sleigh before we can draw too near. We wouldn't ask him to take up residence in the midst of a contaminated people. In our wildest imaginings we wouldn't conjure a king who becomes one of us. But God did.

MAX LUCADO

*"Can anything good come
from Nazareth?" Philip answered, "Come and see."*

JOHN 1:46

Can anything good come out of Nazareth?
Come and see.

See Wilberforce fighting to free slaves
in England. . . .

Journey into the jungles and hear the
drums beating in praise. . . .

Venture into the gulags and dungeons of
the world and hear the songs of the saved
refusing to be silent.

Come and see.

The LORD will be your confidence.

PROVERBS 3:26, NKJV

*T*he temple builders and the Savior seekers. You'll find them both in the same church, on the same pew—at times, even in the same suit. One sees the structure and says, "What a great church." The other sees the Savior and says, "What a great Christ!"

Which do you see?

He will wipe away every tear from their eyes.

REVELATION 21:4

Someday God will wipe away your tears. The same hands that stretched the heavens will touch your cheeks. The same hands that formed the mountains will caress your face. The same hands that curled in agony as the Roman spike cut through will someday cup your face and bush away your tears. Forever.

As many of you as were baptized into Christ have put on Christ.

GALATIANS 3:27, NKJV

You read it right. We have "put on" Christ. When God looks at us He doesn't see us; He sees Christ. We "wear" Him. We are hidden in Him; we are covered by Him. As the song says "Dressed in His righteousness alone, faultless to stand before the throne."

Presumptuous, you say? Sacrilegious? It would be if it were my idea. But it isn't; it's His.

MAX LUCADO

"I have not lost any of the ones you gave me."

JOHN 18:9

*S*atan falls in the presence of Christ. . . .
Satan is powerless against the protection
of Christ.

When Jesus says he will keep you safe,
he means it. Hell will have to get through him
to get to you. Jesus is able to protect you.
When he says he will get you home, he will
get you home.

Because he delights in me, he saved me.

PSALM 18:19

Y ou thought he saved you because of your
good works or good attitude or good looks.
Sorry. If that were the case, your salvation
would be lost when your voice went south or
your works got weak. There are many reasons
God saves you: to bring glory to himself,
to appease his justice, to demonstrate his
sovereignty. But one of the sweetest reasons
God saved you is because he is fond of you.

MAX LUCADO

Love is patient and kind.

1 CORINTHIANS 13:4

*A*gape love cares for others because God has cared for us. *Agape* love goes beyond sentiment and good wishes. Because God loved first, *agape* love responds. Because God was gracious, *agape* love forgives the mistake when the offense is high. *Agape* offers patience when stress is abundant and extends kindness when kindness is rare. Why? Because God offered us both.

Happy are they whose sins
are forgiven, whose wrongs are pardoned.

ROMANS 4:7

To qualify for bankruptcy, you have to admit you are broke. . . .

And to go to heaven, you have to admit you are hellbound.

That's a tough one. . . . Not easy for a decent guy to admit he's a sinner. Hard for a pretty good girl to confess spiritual destitution. . . . If we are saved it is because God rescued us and not because we learned to swim.

MAX LUCADO

Live out this God-created identity the way our Father lives toward us, generously and graciously, even when we're at our worst.

LUKE 6:35, THE MESSAGE

God has proven himself as a faithful father. Now it falls to us to be trusting children. Let God give you what your family doesn't. Let him fill the void others have left. Rely upon him for your affirmation and encouragement.

I am the way, the truth, and the life.
No one comes to the Father except through Me.

JOHN 14:6, NKJV

*J*esus leaves us with two options. Accept him as God, or reject him as a megalomaniac. There is no third alternative. . . .

Call him crazy, or crown him as king. Dismiss him as a fraud, or declare him to be God. Walk away from him, or bow before him, but don't play games with him. Don't call him a great man. Don't list him among decent folk. . . . He is either God or godless. Heaven sent or hell born. All hope or all hype. But nothing in between.

MAX LUCADO

"How long must I stay with you?"

MARK 9 : 19

*H*ow long? "Until the rooster sings and the sweat stings and the mallet rings. . . ."

How long? "Long enough for every sin to so soak my sinless soul that heaven will turn in horror until my swollen lips pronounce the final transaction: 'It is finished.'"

Jesus bore all things, believed all things, hoped all things, and endured all things. Every single one.

*Difficulties are
short-lived.
Rewards are eternal.*

He bore the sin of many, and made intercession for the transgressors.

ISAIAH 53:12, NIV

God is in the thick of things in your world. He has not taken up residence in a distant galaxy. . . . He has not chosen to seclude Himself on a throne in an incandescent castle.

He has drawn near. He has involved Himself in the car pools, heartbreaks, and funeral homes of our day. He is as near to us on Monday as on Sunday. In the school room as in the sanctuary.

MAX LUCADO

Let the loveliness of our Lord, our God,
rest on us, confirming the work that we do.
PSALM 90:17, THE MESSAGE

Anger. It's a peculiar yet predictable emotion. It begins as a drop of water. An irritant. A frustration. Nothing big, just an aggravation. Someone gets your parking place. A waitress is slow and you are in a hurry. Drip. Drip. Drip.

Yet, get enough of these seemingly innocent drops of anger and before long you've got a bucket full of rage. . . .

Now, is that any way to live? . . . Anger never did anyone any good.

Love . . . does not boast, it is not proud.

1 CORINTHIANS 13:4, NIV

*J*esus blasts the top birds of the church, those who roost at the top of the spiritual ladder and spread their plumes of robes, titles, jewelry, and choice seats. Jesus won't stand for it. It's easy to see why. How can I love others if my eyes are only on me? How can I point to God if I'm pointing at me? And, worse still, how can someone see God if I keep fanning my own tail feathers?

Jesus has no room for pecking orders.

MAX LUCADO

Do not fear, from now on you will be catching men.

LUKE 5:10, NASB

Christ . . . doesn't abandon self-confessed schlemiels. Quite the contrary, he enlists them. . . .

Contrary to what you may have been told, Jesus doesn't limit his recruiting to the stout-hearted. The beat up and worn out are prime prospects in his book, and he's been known to climb into boats, bars, and brothels to tell them, "It's not too late to start over."

My grace is enough for you. When you are weak, my power is made perfect in you.

2 CORINTHIANS 12:9

What is grace? It's what someone gives us out of the goodness of his heart, not out of the perfection of ours. The story of grace is the good news that says that when we come, he gives. That's what grace is. . . .

Grace is something you did not expect. It is something you certainly could never earn. But grace is something you'd never turn down.

MAX LUCADO

Life is not defined by what you have, even when you have a lot.

LUKE 12:15, THE MESSAGE

Who you are has nothing to do with the clothes you wear or the car you drive. . . . Heaven does not know you as the fellow with the nice suit or the woman with the big house or the kid with the new bike. Heaven knows your heart. . . .

When God thinks of you, he may see your compassion, your devotion, your tenderness or quick mind, but he doesn't think of your things. . . . And when you think of you, you shouldn't either.

*Behold, this is our God; we have
waited for Him, and He will save us.*

ISAIAH 25:9, NKJV

When people don't listen, remember
Jesus. When tears come, remember Jesus.
When disappointment is your bed partner,
remember Jesus. When fear pitches his tent in
your front yard. When death looms, when
anger simmers, when shame weighs heavily.
Remember Jesus.

Remember the dead called from the grave
with a Galilean accent. Remember the eyes of
God that wept human tears.

He who receives Me receives Him who sent Me.

MATTHEW 10:40, NKJV

*H*ow do you simplify faith? . . .

Simplify your faith by seeking God for yourself. No confusing ceremonies necessary. No mysterious rituals required. No elaborate channels of command or levels of access.

You have a Bible? You can study. You have a heart? You can pray. You have a mind. You can think.

Now we can come fearlessly right into God's presence.

EPHESIANS 3:12, TLV

Christ meets you outside the throne room, takes you by the hand, and walks you into the presence of God. Upon entrance we find grace, not condemnation; mercy, not punishment. . . .

Because we are friends of God's Son, we have entrance to the throne room. . . . This gift is not an occasional visit before God but rather a permanent "access by faith into this grace by which we now stand" (Rom. 5:2, NIV).

Let this mind be in you which was also in Christ Jesus.

PHILIPPIANS 2:5, NKJV

What does it mean to be just like Jesus?
The world has never known a heart so pure,
a character so flawless. His spiritual hearing
was so keen He never missed a heavenly
whisper. His mercy so abundant He never
missed a chance to forgive. No lie left His
lips, no distraction marred His vision.
He touched when others recoiled.
He endured when others quit. Jesus is
the ultimate model for
every person.

Blessed are the merciful, for they will be shown mercy.

MATTHEW 5:7, NIV

*T*he merciful, says Jesus, are shown mercy.
They witness grace. They are blessed because
they are testimonies to a greater goodness.
Forgiving others allows us to see how God has
forgiven us. The dynamic of giving grace is
the key to understanding grace, for it is when
we forgive others that we begin to feel what
God feels.

He is my defender; I will not be defeated.

PSALM 62:6

What does God do when we are in a bind?
. . . He fights for us. He steps into the ring
and points us to our corner and takes over.
"Remain calm; the LORD will fight for you"
(Exod. 14:14).

His job is to fight. Our job is to trust.

Just trust. Not direct. Or question.
Or yank the steering wheel out of his hands.
Our job is to pray and wait.

We can come before God's throne where . . .
we can receive mercy and grace to help us when we need it.

HEBREWS 4:16

*D*on't we need someone to trust who is bigger than we are? Aren't we tired of trusting the people of this earth for understanding? Aren't we weary of trusting the things of this earth for strength? A drowning sailor doesn't call on another drowning sailor for help. . . . He knows he needs someone who is stronger than he is.

Jesus' message is this: I am that person. Trust Me.

*I call you friends, because I have made
known to you everything I heard from my Father.*

JOHN 15:15

John is the only one of the twelve who was at
the cross. He came to say good-bye. By his
own admission he hadn't quite put the pieces
together yet. But that didn't really matter.
As far as he was concerned, his closest friend
was in trouble and he came to help. . . .

John teaches us that the . . . greatest webs
of loyalty are spun, not with airtight theologies
or foolproof philosophies, but with friendships;
stubborn, selfless, joyful friendships.

The payoff for meekness and Fear-of-GOD
is plenty and honor and a satisfying life.
PROVERBS 22:4, THE MESSAGE

*T*rue humility is not thinking lowly of
yourself but thinking accurately of yourself.
The humble heart does not say, "I can't do
anything." But rather, "I can't do everything.
I know my part and am happy to do it."

As you received Christ Jesus the Lord, so continue to live in him.

COLOSSIANS 2:6

Struggling with life's difficulties makes us a little wiser, a little more capable, enabling us to comfort others who experience pain.

Any difficulties we face in life are short-lived; all rewards are eternal. A divine inheritance will be our reward for faithfulness to our heavenly Father.

Give all your worries to him, because he cares about you.

1 PETER 5:7

Maybe you don't want to trouble God with your hurts. *After all, he's got famines and pestilence and wars; he won't care about my little struggles,* you think. Why don't you let him decide that? He cared enough about a wedding to provide the wine. He cared enough about Peter's tax payment to give him a coin. He cared enough about the woman at the well to give her answers.

MAX LUCADO

Come to me, . . . and you will find rest for your lives.

MATTHEW 11:28-29

*C*ome to me. . . .

The people came. . . .They brought him the burdens of their existence, and he gave them not religion, not doctrine, not systems, but rest. . . .

They found anchor points for their storm-tossed souls. And they found that Jesus was the only man to walk God's earth who claimed to have an answer for man's burdens. "Come to me."

"I am the Holy One, and I am among you."

HOSEA 11:9

You can claim courage from God's promises. May I give a few examples?

When you are confused: "'I know what I am planning for you,' says the LORD. 'I have good plans for you, not plans to hurt you'" (Jer. 29:11).

On those nights when you wonder where God is: "I am the Holy One, and I am among you" (Hos. 11:9).

God, examine me and know
my heart. . . . Lead me on the road to everlasting life.

PSALM 139:23—24

You don't have to be like the world to have an impact on the world. You don't have to be like the crowd to change the crowd. You don't have to lower yourself down to their level to lift them up to your level. Holiness doesn't seek to be odd. Holiness seeks to be like God.

Each of us is an original.

GALATIANS 5:26, THE MESSAGE

*T*here are certain things you can do that no one else can. Perhaps it is parenting, or constructing houses, or encouraging the discouraged. There are things that *only* you can do, and you are alive to do them. In the great orchestra we call life, you have an instrument and a song, and you owe it to God to play them both sublimely.

MAX LUCADO

I have chosen the way of truth; I have set my heart on your laws.

PSALM 119:30, NIV

Think about it. There are many things in life we can't choose. We can't, for example, choose the weather. We can't control the economy. We can't choose whether or not we are born with a big nose or blue eyes or a lot of hair. . . . But we can choose where we spend eternity. The big choice, God leaves to us.

OCTOBER 23

Teach me how to live to please you, because you're my God.
PSALM 143:8, THE MESSAGE

If God has called you to be a Martha,
then serve! Remind the rest of us that there is
evangelism in feeding the poor and there is
worship in nursing the sick.

If God has called you to be a Mary,
then worship! Remind the rest of us that we
don't have to be busy to be holy. Urge us with
your example to put down our clipboards and
megaphones and be quiet in worship.

When you talk, do not say harmful things, but say what people need—words that will help others become stronger.

EPHESIANS 4:29

You have the ability, with your words, to make a person stronger. Your words are to their soul what a vitamin is to their body.

Do not withhold encouragement from the discouraged. Do not keep affirmation from the beaten down! Speak words that make people stronger. Believe in them as God has believed in you.

Be a worker who is not ashamed
and who uses the true teaching in the right way.

2 TIMOTHY 2:15

*T*imothy never had another teacher like Paul.
The world has never had another teacher like
Paul. He was convinced of two facts—he was
once lost but then saved. He spent a lifetime
telling every person who would listen.

In the end it cost him everything. For in
the end, all he had was his faith. But in the
end, his faith was all he needed.

MAX LUCADO

Christ carried our sins in his body on the cross.

1 PETER 2:24

*I*n an act that broke the heart of the Father, yet honored the holiness of heaven, sin-purging judgment flowed over the sinless Son of the ages.

And heaven gave earth her finest gift. The Lamb of God who took away the sin of the world.

"My God, my God, why did you abandon me?" Why did Christ scream those words?

So you'll never have to.

The fear of the LORD, that is wisdom.

JOB 28:28, NKJV

*A*mbition is that grit in the soul that creates disenchantment with the ordinary and puts the dare into dreams.

But left unchecked it becomes an insatiable addiction to power and prestige; a roaring hunger for achievement that devours people as a lion devours an animal, leaving behind only the skeletal remains of relationships. . . .

God won't tolerate it.

Don't judge other people or you will be judged.

MATTHEW 7:1

*R*ather than see the man born blind as an opportunity for discussion, Jesus saw him as an opportunity for God. Why was he blind? "So God's power could be shown in him" (John 9:3).

What a perspective! The man wasn't a victim of fate; he was a miracle waiting to happen. Jesus didn't label him. He helped him. Jesus was more concerned about the future than the past.

"We were eyewitnesses of his majesty."

2 PETER 1:16, RSV

God came near. To be seen.

And . . . those who saw him were never the same. "We saw his glory" exclaimed one follower. "We were eyewitnesses of his majesty," whispered a martyr. . . .

Christianity, in its purest form, is nothing more than seeing Jesus. Christian service, in its purest form, is nothing more than imitating him whom we see.

MAX LUCADO

"Speak, LORD. I am your servant and I am listening."

1 SAMUEL 3:9

We expect God to speak through peace,
but sometimes he speaks through pain. . . .

We think we hear him in the sunrise,
but he is also heard in the darkness.

We listen for him in triumph, but he
speaks even more distinctly through tragedy.

I am the God of your father Abraham;
do not fear, for I am with you.

GENESIS 26:24, NKJV

*H*ope is not what you expect; it's what you would never dream. . . . It's Abraham adjusting his bifocals so he can see not his grandson, but his son. . . .

Hope is not a granted wish or a favor performed; no, it's far greater than that. It's a zany, unpredictable dependence on a God who loves to surprise us out of our socks and be there in the flesh to see our reaction.

MAX LUCADO

NOVEMBER

God's love

never ceases.

The LORD said, "I have loved you."

MALACHI 1:2

*F*ather, your love never ceases. Never. Though we spurn you, ignore you, disobey you, you will not change. Our evil cannot diminish your love. Our goodness cannot increase it. Our faith does not earn it anymore than our stupidity jeopardizes it. You don't love us less if we fail. You don't love us more if we succeed.

Your love never ceases.

I came to give life—life in all its fullness.

JOHN 10:10

Jesus is no run-of-the-mill messiah. His story was extraordinary. He called himself divine, yet allowed a minimum-wage Roman soldier to drive a nail into his wrist. He demanded purity, yet stood for the rights of a repentant whore. He called men to march, yet refused to allow them to call him King. He sent men into all the world, yet equipped them with only bended knees and memories of a resurrected carpenter.

You were chosen to tell about the wonderful acts
of God, who called you out of darkness into his wonderful light.

1 PETER 2:9

*U*ncontrolled anger won't better our
world, but sympathetic understanding will.
Once we see the world and ourselves for what
we are, we can help. Once we understand
ourselves we begin to operate not from a
posture of anger but of compassion and
concern. We look at the world not with
bitter frowns but with extended hands.
We realize that the lights are out and a lot of
people are stumbling in the darkness. So we
light candles.

*The master will dress himself to serve and tell
the servants to sit at the table, and he will serve them.*

LUKE 12:37

The humble heart honors others.

Again, is Jesus not our example?
Content to be known as a carpenter.
Happy to be mistaken for the gardener.
He served his followers by washing their feet.
He serves us by doing the same. Each morning
he gifts us with beauty. Each Sunday he calls
us to his table. Each moment he dwells in our
hearts. . . . If Jesus is so willing to honor us,
can we not do the same for others?

*Those who believe in me, even though
they die like everyone else, will live again.*

JOHN 11: 25, NLT

Mourning is not disbelieving. Flooded eyes don't represent a faithless heart. A person can enter a cemetery Jesus-certain of life after death and still have a Twin Tower crater in the heart. Christ did. He wept, and he knew he was ten minutes from seeing a living Lazarus!

And his tears give you permission to shed your own. . . . So grieve, but don't grieve like those who don't know the rest of this story.

MAX LUCADO

I've already run for dear life straight to the arms of GOD.

PSALM 11:1, THE MESSAGE

I've noticed that those who serve God most joyfully are the ones who know him most personally. Those who are quickest to speak about Jesus are those who realize how great has been their own redemption.

God is an exalted friend, a holy Father, an elevated King. How do we approach him— as king, as father, or as friend? The answer: yes!

It is by grace you have been saved,
through faith—and this not from yourselves, it is the gift of God.

EPHESIANS 2:8, NIV

With his own pierced hands, Jesus created a pasture for the soul. He tore out the thorny underbrush of condemnation. He pried loose the huge boulders of sin. In their place he planted seeds of grace and dug ponds of mercy.

And he invites us to rest there. Can you imagine the satisfaction in the heart of the shepherd when, with work completed, he sees his sheep rest in the tender grass?

MAX LUCADO

If they could be made God's people by what they did, God's gift of grace would not really be a gift.

ROMANS 11:6

To whom does God offer his gift? To the brightest? The most beautiful or the most charming? No. His gift is for us all—beggars and bankers, clergy and clerks, judges and janitors. All God's children.

And he wants us so badly, he'll take us in any condition—"as is" reads the tag on our collars. . . .

He wants us *now*.

EVERYDAY BLESSINGS

I will live with them and walk with them. And I will be their God, and they will be my people.

2 CORINTHIANS 6:16

Those who saw Jesus—really saw Him—knew there was something different. At His touch blind beggars saw. At His command crippled legs walked. At His embrace empty lives filled with vision.

He fed thousands with one basket.
He stilled a storm with one command.
He raised the dead with one proclamation.
He changed lives with one request.

*He who believes in Me, as the Scripture
has said, out of his heart will flow rivers of living water.*

JOHN 7:38, NKJV

*R*emember the words of Jesus to the
Samaritan woman? "The water I give will
become a spring of water gushing up inside
that person, giving eternal life" (John 4:14).
Jesus offers, not a singular drink of water,
but a perpetual artesian well! And the well
isn't a hole in your backyard but the Holy
Spirit of God in your heart.

Our old life died with Christ on the cross
so that our sinful selves would have no power over us.

Romans 6:6

*T*hink of it this way. Sin put you in prison. Sin locked you behind the bars of guilt and shame and deception and fear. Sin did nothing but shackle you to the wall of misery. Then Jesus came and paid your bail. He served your time; he satisfied the penalty and set you free. Christ died, and when you cast your lot with him, your old self died too.

When Jesus died, you died to sin's claim on your life. You are free.

*He has covered me with clothes of
salvation and wrapped me with a coat of goodness.*

ISAIAH 61:10

Do you ever feel unnoticed? New clothes and styles may help for a while. But if you want permanent change, learn to see yourself as God sees you: "He has covered me with clothes of salvation and wrapped me with a coat of goodness, like a bridegroom dressed for his wedding, like a bride dressed in jewels" (Isa. 61:10).

Allow God's love to change the way you look at you.

They sinned against me, but I will wash away that sin.

JEREMIAH 33:8

*T*he next time you see or think of the one who broke your heart, look twice. As you look at his face, look also for His face—the face of the One who forgave you. Look into the eyes of the King who wept when you pleaded for mercy. Look into the face of the Father who gave you grace when no one else gave you a chance. . . . And then, because God has forgiven you more than you'll ever be called on to forgive in another, set your enemy— and yourself—free.

MAX LUCADO

No one has ever imagined what
God has prepared for those who love him.

1 CORINTHIANS 2:9

*A*nything you imagine is inadequate.
Anything anyone imagines is inadequate.
No one has come close. No one. Think of
all the songs about heaven. All the artists'
portrayals. All the lessons preached, poems
written, and chapters drafted.

When it comes to describing heaven,
we are all happy failures.

When you were in trouble, you called,
and I saved you. I answered you with thunder.

PSALM 81:7

God is as creative as he is relentless. The same hand that sent manna to Israel sent Uzzah to his death. The same hand that set the children free from Israel also sent them captive to Babylon. Both kind and stern. Tender and tough. Faithfully firm. Patiently urgent. Eagerly tolerant. Softly shouting. Gently thundering.

MAX LUCADO

This is the true grace of God. Stand strong in that grace.

1 PETER 5:12

*U*p the hill we trudge. Weary, wounded hearts wrestling with unresolved mistakes. Sighs of anxiety. Tears of frustration. Words of rationalization. Moans of doubt. . . .

Jesus stands on life's most barren hill and waits with outstretched, nail-pierced hands. A "crazy, holy grace" it has been called. A type of grace that doesn't hold up to logic. But then . . . grace doesn't have to be logical. If it did, it wouldn't be grace.

You are . . . God's own possession.

1 PETER 2:9

God loves you simply because He has chosen to do so.

He loves you when you don't feel lovely.

He loves you when no one else loves you.

Others may abandon you, divorce you, and ignore you, but God will love you. Always. No matter what.

MAX LUCADO

Being kind to the poor is like lending to the LORD; he will reward you for what you have done.

PROVERBS 19:17

When you take food to the poor, that's an act of worship. When you give a word of kindness to someone who needs it, that's an act of worship. When you write someone a letter to encourage them or sit down and open your Bible with someone to teach them, that's an act of worship.

GOD always does what he says,
and is gracious in everything he does.

PSALM 145:13, THE MESSAGE

God never gives up.

When Moses said, "Here I am, send Aaron," God didn't give up. . . . When Peter worshiped him at the supper and cursed him at the fire, he didn't give up. . . .

So, the next time doubt walks into your life remember the cross, where in holy blood is written the promise, "God would give up his only son before he'd give up on you."

MAX LUCADO

*He makes me to lie down in
green pastures; He leads me beside the still waters.*

PSALM 23:2, NKJV

Note the two pronouns preceding the two verbs. *He* makes me . . . *He* leads me. . . .

Who is in charge? The shepherd. The shepherd selects the trail and prepares the pasture. The sheep's job—our job—is to watch the shepherd.

We know that in everything
God works for the good of those who love him.

ROMANS 8:28

*E*verything? Everything. Chicken-hearted
disciples. A two-timing Judas. A pierced side.
Spineless Pharisees. A hardhearted high
priest. In everything God worked. I dare you
to find one element of the cross that he did
not manage for good or recycle for
symbolism. Give it a go. I think you'll find
what I found—every dark detail was actually a
golden moment in the cause of Christ.

Can't he do the same for you?

"The work God wants you to do is this: Believe the One he sent."

JOHN 6:29

"What are the things God wants us to do?" (John 6:28). . . . What is the work he wants us to do? Pray more? Give more? Study? Travel? . . .

What is the work he seeks? Just believe. Believe the One he sent. "The work God wants you to do is this: Believe the One he sent."

Behold, I stand at the door and knock.

REVELATION 3:20, NASB

*J*esus always knocks before entering.

He doesn't have to. He owns your heart.

If anyone has the right to barge in,
Christ does.

But He doesn't.

That gentle tap you hear? It's Christ.

MAX LUCADO

Christ brings a new agreement from God to his people.

HEBREWS 9:15

*T*here was nothing inferior about the Jewish religion. It was given by God and designed by God. Every principle, rule, and ritual had a wealth of meaning. The Old Testament served as a faithful guide for thousands of people over thousands of years. It was the best offered to man.

But when Christ came, the best got better. . . . It's not that the old law was bad, it's just that the new law—salvation by faith in Christ—is better.

You made me and formed me with your hands.
Give me understanding so I can learn your commands.

PSALM 119:73

God has gifted you with talents. He has done the same to your neighbor. If you concern yourself with your neighbor's talents, you will neglect yours. But if you concern yourself with yours, you could inspire both.

MAX LUCADO

He was born to be a man and became like a servant.

PHILIPPIANS 2:7

*H*oliday travel. It isn't easy. Then why do we do it? Why cram the trunks and endure the airports? You know the answer. We love to be with the ones we love. . . .

May I remind you? So does God. . . . Between him and us there was a distance— a great span. And he couldn't bear it. He couldn't stand it. So he did something about it. "He gave up his place with God and made himself nothing" (Phil. 2:6).

I will be merciful to their unrighteousness,
and their sins . . . I will remember no more.

Wow! Now, *that* is a remarkable promise.
God doesn't just forgive, He forgets.
He erases the board. He destroys the
evidence. He burns the microfilm. He clears
the computer.

He doesn't remember my mistakes.
For all the things he does do, this is one thing
he refuses to do. He refuses to keep
a list of my wrongs.

MAX LUCADO

"If only you knew the free gift of God."

JOHN 4:10 .

When Jesus washed the disciples' feet, he was washing ours; when he calmed their storms, he was calming yours; when he forgave Peter, he was forgiving all the penitent. . . .

He hasn't changed. . . .

The gift and the Giver. If you know them, you know all you need.

"He really was the Son of God!"

MATTHEW 27:54

Six hours one Friday. . . . What do these six hours signify? . . .

For the life blackened with failure, that Friday means forgiveness.

For the heart scarred with futility, that Friday means purpose.

And for the soul looking into this side of the tunnel of death, that Friday means deliverance.

MAX LUCADO

*In Him we have redemption
through His blood, the forgiveness of sins.*

EPHESIANS 1:7, NKJV

The blood of Christ does not cover your sins, conceal your sins, postpone your sins, or diminish your sins. It takes away your sins, once and for all time.

Jesus allows your mistakes to be lost in His perfection.

DECEMBER

God came near.

Our high priest is able to understand our weaknesses.

HEBREWS 4:15

When God chose to reveal himself, he did so (surprise of surprises) through a human body. The tongue that called forth the dead was a human one. The hand that touched the leper had dirt under its nails. The feet upon which the woman wept were calloused and dusty. And his tears . . . oh, don't miss the tears . . . they came from a heart as broken as yours or mine ever has been.

MAX LUCADO

With your very own hands
you formed me; now breathe your wisdom over me.

PSALM 119:73, THE MESSAGE

Listen closely. Jesus' love does not depend upon what we do for him. Not at all. In the eyes of the King, you have value simply because you are. You don't have to look nice or perform well. Your value is inborn.

You are valuable . . . not because of what you do or what you have done, but simply because you are. Remember that.

His name will be . . . Prince of Peace.

I S A I A H 9 : 6

*H*eaven opened herself and placed her most precious one in a human womb.

The omnipotent, in one instant, made himself breakable. He who had been spirit became pierceable. He who was larger than the universe became an embryo. And he who sustains the world with a word chose to be dependent upon the nourishment of a young girl.

God had come near.

Do nothing from selfishness or empty conceit.

PHILIPPIANS 2:3, NASB

*T*he word . . . for *selfishness* shares a root form
with the words *strife* and *contentious*. It suggests a
self-preoccupation that hurts others. . . .
*Selfishness is an obsession with self that excludes others,
hurting everyone.*

Looking after your personal interests is
proper life management. Doing so to the
exclusion of the rest of the world
is selfishness.

You are my God. . . . Lead me on level ground.

PSALM 143:10

Can you imagine the outcome if a parent honored each request of each child during a trip? We'd inch our bloated bellies from one ice-cream store to the next. . . .

Can you imagine the chaos if God indulged each of ours?

MAX LUCADO

I have it all planned out—
plans to take care of you, not abandon you.

JEREMIAH 29:11, THE MESSAGE

We have a Father who is filled with compassion, a feeling Father who hurts when his children hurt. We serve a God who says that even when we're under pressure and feel like nothing is going to go right, he's waiting for us, to embrace us whether we succeed or fail. . . .

He comes into our hearts like a gentle lamb, not a roaring lion.

God's grace that can save everyone has come.

Titus 2:11

As moments go, that one appeared no different than any others. . . . It came and went. . . . It was one of the countless moments that have marked time since eternity became measurable.

But in reality, that particular moment was like none other. For through that segment of time a spectacular thing occurred. God became a man. While the creatures of earth walked unaware, Divinity arrived.

Max Lucado

God . . . gives grace to the humble.

1 PETER 5:5

The apostle Paul was saved through a personal visit from Jesus. He was carried into the heavens and had the ability to raise the dead. But when he introduced himself, he mentioned none of these. He simply said, "I, Paul, am God's slave" (Titus 1:1, THE MESSAGE). . .

God loves humility.

You are all around me—in front
and in back—and have put your hand on me.

PSALM 139:5

We wonder with so many miraculous
testimonies around us, how we could escape
God. But somehow we do. We live in an art
gallery of divine creativity and yet are content
to gaze only at the carpet.

The next time you hear a baby laugh or
see an ocean wave, take note. Pause and listen
as His Majesty whispers ever so gently,
"I'm here."

*His mercy is everlasting,
and His truth endures to all generations.*

PSALM 100:5, NKJV

*J*esus died . . . on purpose. No surprise. No hesitation. No faltering. . . .

The journey to the cross didn't begin in Jericho. It didn't begin in Galilee. It didn't begin in Nazarath. It didn't even begin in Bethlehem. The journey to the cross began long before. As the echo of the crunching of the fruit was still sounding in the garden, Jesus was leaving for Calvary.

I will meditate on the glorious splendor
of Your majesty, and on Your wondrous works.

PSALM 145:5, NKJV

*H*as it been a while since you stared at the heavens is speechless amazement? Has it been awhile since you realized God's divinity . . . ?

If it has, then you need to know something. He is still there. He hasn't left. Under all those papers and books and reports and years. In the midst of all those voices and faces and memories and pictures, He is still there.

MAX LUCADO

We shall not all sleep, but we shall all be changed—
in a moment, in the twinkling of an eye, at the last trumpet.

1 CORINTHIANS 15:51–52, NKJV

When Jesus went home he left the back door open. As a result, "we will all be changed—in a moment, in the twinkling of an eye."

The first moment of transformation went unnoticed by the world. But you can bet your sweet September the second one won't. The next time you use the phrase "just a moment . . ." remember that's all the time it will take to change this world.

Oh magnify the LORD with me,
and let us exalt His name together.

PSALM 34:3, NASB

Worship is the act of magnifying God.
Enlarging our vision of Him. Stepping into
the cockpit to see where He sits and observe
how He works. Of course, His size doesn't
change, but our perception of Him does.
As we draw nearer, He seems larger. Isn't that
what we need? A *big* view of God?

MAX LUCADO

"We were . . . eyewitnesses of His majesty."

2 PETER 1:16, NKJV

Have you seen Jesus? Those who first did were never the same.

"My Lord and my God!" cried Thomas.

"I have seen the Lord," exclaimed Mary Magdalene.

"We have seen His glory," declared John.

But Peter said it best. "We were eyewitnesses of His majesty."

God is at work within you, helping you want
to obey him, and then helping you do what he wants.

PHILIPPIANS 2:13, TLB

As a result of being saved, what do we do?
We obey God with deep reverence and shrink
back from all that might displease Him.
Practically put, we love our neighbor and
refrain from gossip. We refuse to cheat on
taxes and spouses and do our best to love
people who are tough to love. Do we do this
in order to be saved? No. These are the good
things that result from being saved.

MAX LUCADO

Glory to God in the highest!

LUKE 2:14, NKJV

For the shepherds it wasn't enough to see the angels. You'd think it would have been. Night sky shattered with light. Stillness erupting with song. Simple shepherds roused from their sleep and raised to their feet by a choir of angels: "Glory to God in the highest!" Never had these men seen such splendor.

But it wasn't enough to see the angels. The shepherds wanted to see the one who sent the angels.

We know and rely on the love God has for us.

1 JOHN 4:16, NIV

The secret to loving is living loved. . . .

Does bumping into certain people leave you brittle, breakable, and fruitless? . . . If so, your love may be grounded in the wrong soil. It may be rooted in their love (which is fickle) or in your resolve to love (which is frail). John urges us to "rely on the love *God* has for us" (1 John 4:16, NIV). He alone is the power source.

MAX LUCADO

*Everything [God] does is good
and fair; all his orders can be trusted.*

*T*here is not a hint of one person who was
afraid to draw near Jesus. There were those
who mocked Him. There were those who were
envious of Him. There were those who
misunderstood Him. There were those who
revered Him. But there was not one person
who considered Him too holy, too divine,
or too celestial to touch. *There was not one
person who was reluctant to approach Him for fear of
being rejected.*

I came to give life—life in all its fullness.

JOHN 10:10

An ordinary night with ordinary sheep and ordinary shepherds. And were it not for a God who loves to hook an "extra" on the front of the ordinary, the night would have gone unnoticed. The sheep would have been forgotten, and the shepherds would have slept the night away.

But God dances amidst the common. And that night he did a waltz. . . . The night was ordinary no more.

The steadfast love of the LORD never ceases.

LAMENTATIONS 3:22, NRSV

Our God is not aloof—he's not so far above us that he can't see and understand our problems. Jesus isn't a God who stayed on the mountaintop—he's a Savior who came down and lived and worked with the people. Everywhere he went, the crowds followed, drawn together by the magnet that was— and is—the Savior.

The life of Jesus Christ is a message of hope.

If your faith is as big as a mustard seed, you can say to this mountain, "Move from here to there," and it will move.

MATTHEW 17:20

Don't measure the size of the mountain; talk to the One who can move it. Instead of carrying the world on your shoulders, talk to the One who holds the universe on his. Hope is a look away.

Happy are the people . . . who walk,
O LORD, in the light of your countenance.

PSALM 89:15, NRSV

Jesus didn't fit the Jews' notion of a Messiah, and so, rather than change their notion, they dismissed him. . . .

They expected lights and kings and chariots from heaven. What they got was sandals and sermons and a Galilean accent.

And so, some missed him. And so, some miss him still.

Nothing . . . in the whole world
will ever be able to separate us from the love of God.

ROMANS 8:39

*E*ven after generations of people had spit in His face, God still loved them. After a nation of chosen ones had stripped Him naked and ripped His incarnated flesh, He still died for them. And even today, after billions have chosen to prostitute themselves before the pimps of power, fame, and wealth, He still waits for them. . . .

Only God could love like that.

MAX LUCADO

He . . . loads me with love and mercy.

PSALM 103:4

*I*t's time to let God's love cover all things in your life. All secrets. All hurts. All hours of evil, minutes of worry.

Discover along with the psalmist: "He . . . loads me with love and mercy." Picture a giant dump truck full of love. There you are behind it. God lifts the bed until the love starts to slide. Slowly at first, then down, down, down until you are hidden, buried, and covered in his love.

She brought forth her firstborn Son, and wrapped
Him in swaddling cloths, and laid Him in a manger.

LUKE 2:7, NKJV

The virgin birth is more, much more, than a Christmas story; it is a picture of how close Christ will come to you. The first stop on his itinerary was a womb. Where will God go to touch the world? Look deep within Mary for an answer.

Better still, look deep within yourself. What he did with Mary, he offers to us! He issues a Mary-level invitation to all his children. "If you'll let me, I'll move in!"

His kingdom will never end.

LUKE 1:33

*S*omehow Mary knows she is holding God. *So this is he.* She remembers the words of the angel. "His kingdom will never end."

He looks like anything but a king. His face is prunish and red. His cry, though strong and healthy, is still the helpless and piercing cry of a baby. And he is absolutely dependent upon Mary for his well-being.

Majesty in the midst of the mundane.

[They] put him to death by nailing him to a cross.
But this was God's plan which he had made long ago.

ACTS 2:23

*T*he cross wasn't a tragic surprise. Calvary was not a knee-jerk response to a world plummeting toward destruction. It wasn't a patch-up job or a stop-gap measure. . . .

The moment the forbidden fruit touched the lips of Eve, the shadow of a cross appeared on the horizon. And between that moment and the moment the man with the mallet placed the spike against the wrist of God, a master plan was fulfilled.

MAX LUCADO

I look at your heavens, which you made with your fingers. I see the moon and stars, which you created.

PSALM 8:3

We serve the God who designed the universe and set our world in motion. But those hands that hung the stars in the heavens also wiped away the tears of the widow and the leper. And they will wipe away your tears as well.

Carefully build yourselves up in this most holy faith by praying in the Holy Spirit, staying right at the center of God's love.

JUDE 20, THE MESSAGE

*I*magine considering every moment as a potential time of communion with God. By the time your life is over, you will have spent six months at stoplights, eight months opening junk mail, a year and a half looking for lost stuff . . . , and a whopping five years standing in various lines.

Why don't you give these moments to God?

MAX LUCADO

I will live in the house of the LORD forever.

PSALM 23:6

When David says, "I will live in the house of the LORD forever," he's saying simply that he never wants to step away from God. He craves to remain in the aura, in the atmosphere, in the awareness that he is in God's house, wherever he is. . . .

God wants to be the one in whom "we live and move and have our being" (Acts 17:28, NIV).

Your word is like a lamp for my feet and a light for my path.

PSALM 119:105

God isn't going to let you see the distant scene. So you might as well quit looking for it. He promises a lamp unto our feet, not a crystal ball into the future. We do not need to know what will happen tomorrow. We only need to know He leads us and we will find grace to help us when we need it.

MAX LUCADO

Grateful acknowledgment is made to the following publishers for permission to reprint this copyrighted material. All copyrights are held by the author, Max Lucado.

Lucado, Max. *And the Angels Were Silent* (Nashville: W Publishing Group, 2003).

———*The Applause of Heaven* (Nashville: W. Publishing Group, 1990).

Max Lucado, Michael W. Smith, Third Day, *Come Together & Worship* (Nashville: J. Countryman, 2003)

Max Lucado, *A Gentle Thunder* (Nashville: W Publishing Group, 1995).

———*He Chose the Nails* (Nashville: W Publishing Group, 2000).

———*In the Eye of the Storm* (Nashville: W Publishing Group, 1991).

———*In the Grip of Grace* (Nashville: W. Publishing Group, 1996).

Max Lucado, General Editor, *The Inspirational Study Bible* (Nashville: W Publishing Group, 1995)

———*God Came Near.* (Nashville: W Publishing Group, 2003).

———*Just Like Jesus* (Nashville: W Publishing Group, 1998).

———*No Wonder They Call Him the Savior* (Nashville: W Publishing Group, 2003).

———*Six Hours One Friday* (Nashville: W Publishing Group, 2003).

———*Traveling Light* (Nashville: W Publishing Group, 2000).

———*When Christ Comes* (Nashville: W Publishing, 1999).